CULTIVATING
LEADERSHIP

HOW GREAT LEADERS MAKE A
DIFFERENCE, ONE HOTEL AT A TIME

CULTIVATING LEADERSHIP

JO-ANNE C. HILL

DEDICATION

*This book is dedicated to the wisest person
I have ever known — my Mother, Jean Hill. She was
always full of great advice based on common sense
and usually peppered with a quick wit. Her mantra
to 'just get it done' led her to calmly and quietly do
what needed to be done in times of crisis and joy.
She lived a life of selfless service that knew no bounds.*

Copyright © 2018, Jo-Anne C. Hill

All rights reserved. No part of this book may be reproduced in any form or by any electronic or mechanical means, including information storage and retrieval systems, without permission in writing from the author, except by reviewers, who may quote brief passages in a review.

ISBN-13: 978-1984094957

Book designer: Paul Hodgson
Spot illustrations: Shelagh Armstrong
Content editor: Helen Wilkie, mhwilkiebooks.com
Copy editor: Alexandra Dodds, Alexandraldodds@gmail.com
Proofing editor: Joanne Haskins, thinkcom.ca
Printer: CreateSpace
To order additional copies of this book, visit: www.amazon.com

For more information about Jo-Anne Hill and/or
JH Hospitality Consulting, visit www.jhhospitality.com

CONTENTS

Introduction // 9

– 1 –
Leadership in Action // 15

– 2 –
What Makes a Great Hotel Leader? // 25

– 3 –
What Is Great Service? // 37

– 4 –
Empathy and Customer Service // 45

– 5 –
Leadership and the Customer Experience // 53

– 6 –
Shifting the Paradigm:
Leading an Employee-Centric Hotel // 63

– 7 –
Getting Everyone on the Same Page:
The Importance of Culture in an Organization // 77

– 8 –
The Nuts and Bolts:
Organizational Structure, Processes, and Standards // 87

– 9 –
Financial Return // 97

– 10 –
Why Is This Important? Why Now? // 105

> "Why is it that hotels value their hangers more than their employees?"

CHIP CONLEY

PEAK: HOW GREAT COMPANIES GET
THEIR MOJO FROM MASLOW[1]

INTRODUCTION

CULTIVATING LEADERSHIP: HOW GREAT LEADERS MAKE A DIFFERENCE, ONE HOTEL AT A TIME

It's an adage in the hotel world: take care of employees, and they will take care of the guests. I first heard it when I was a sales manager at a Four Seasons hotel in the '80s and marveled at the simplicity of the equation. Now on reflection, I realize that in those days I had the privilege of working with one of the best bosses of my career, Tom Norwalk, and a terrific general manager, Ruy Paes Braga, who, sadly, passed away recently. We all worked extremely hard, yet there was a camaraderie that I haven't experienced since.

At the time, I took for granted that great leaders were fair, empathetic, and compassionate all while providing gracious hospitality to guests and employees alike — just as Tom and Ruy were. Unfortunately, as I've since learned, that's not always the case.

Thirty years later, leaders still need to be reminded of this concept of 'taking care of the employee,' even to the point of providing examples of what that looks like in action. The unspoken part of the equation is that when guests are taken care of, feel wanted, have their needs met and their expectations exceeded, they become more loyal to the hotel. They spend more money while they are there. They tell all their friends about the experience, becoming evangelists for the hotel, and they are more likely to return themselves.

This means that employee care can be directly related to increased revenue and profitability. To some hotel owners, corporate executives, or even hotel general managers, this shift in focus — this idea of allocating time and money to increase leaders' empathy and employees' wellbeing, rather than spending resources on guest-facing programs and amenities — can seem counterintuitive. In the long run, though, owners and management companies who are prepared to make this investment will see the financial rewards. That is what this book is about.

SO WHY ANOTHER BOOK ON LEADERSHIP?

Despite all the books, training courses, and feedback sessions on leadership, Gallup results continue to report the stagnating rate of employee engagement across North America.[2] Employees leave their jobs primarily because their boss is ineffective, whether that's because they are unable to provide clear guidance and direction, treat employees with respect and fairness, or give appropriate feedback or recognition. Staff turnover has a direct financial impact, including recruitment costs and ramp-up as well as training expenses for new employees, not to mention gaps in service before a new employee is hired and brought up to speed.

THE SOFT, BUT ESSENTIAL, SKILLS OF LEADERSHIP

In my thirty-plus years of experience and observation in the hotel industry, working in locations around the world, I have come to realize that it's attributes such as graciousness, empathy, compassion, trust, and integrity that truly separate the average leaders from the exceptional and that these attributes can be developed. Of course, leaders also need to have a vision and an ability to communicate and handle tough conversations, but those who can activate their hearts are the ones who bring winning teams together.

WHY NOW?

There are five key reasons why, now more than ever, hotels need great leaders who have developed these skills.

1. **Guest expectations have risen exponentially, resulting in customers demanding more value for their dollar than ever before.**

TripAdvisor started in 2000 and has grown to become the most prolific and important customer-feedback voice for hotels in North America. Each month, sixty-five million visitors view the site for reviews on hotels, restaurants, and travel destinations around the world.

Results on the site are often discussed at daily hotel meetings, and time is spent determining not only how to respond to the comments, but the cause of the issues, especially when the same problem comes up repeatedly.

With more resources at their disposal when making reservations at a hotel, including an easy online access to impartial reviews, customers have a clear view of what they are getting during the decision-making process. This has made customers more aware of their options as well as what they should be expecting.

From a pricing perspective, the arrival of Expedia in 1996 changed the landscape of hotel rates. As they could quickly and easily check a variety of options, customers began demanding transparency, forcing hotels to lift the veil on the opaque world of hotel pricing. Potential guests insisted rates be logical and fairly priced, based on the product and compared to the competition. Otherwise, customers would vote with their feet and go elsewhere.

These transparencies simultaneously gave customers more awareness and higher expectations of their hotel stay. Today, hotel leaders need to be in tune with their guests' changing needs. At the same time, they must be able to calibrate their resources, such as employee training and systems, to lead through the minefield of customer expectations.

2. **Increased competition means that, more than ever before, it is critical for organizations to *differentiate* themselves from their competitors.**

Within the last twenty years, arguably the most volatile period in recent US history, there has been an exponential increase in US lodging inventory. As more hotels come online, the majority of which are geographically clustered in major cities and popular resort destinations, hotel leaders are faced with finding unique ways to differentiate their hotel from the competition. This goes beyond the traditional areas of design and product, since customers are now demanding more than the basics at every hotel, not only at luxury properties.

3. ***Customers are attracted* to organizations that articulate who they are and why they are in business.**

This is one of the reasons for Four Seasons' success. Isadore Sharp, founder and chairman, espoused the golden rule as one of the foundations of the company from its beginning in 1961: treat others as you would want to be treated. That ideology, combined with the service excellence the organization pioneered, such as providing bathrobes in all rooms, gave guests a window into the soul of the organization.

Customers are more likely to buy a product or service when the organization's soul is clearly seen, and even more so when they share a similar belief system.

4. **Hotel *revenue and profitability increase* when customers are satisfied.**

Research shows that satisfied guests spend more and return more often. Good leaders know how to train employees to provide extraordinary service so that every guest has a positive experience throughout their stay. Great leaders ensure such training as well as create an environment where care and compassion are seamless for both guests and employees.

5. **When faced with the choice between a cold and uncaring leader and one who provides a respectful, trusting, empathetic, and compassionate environment, *discerning employees will gravitate* to the latter.**

Great leaders attract great employees, so when there is an opening on the team, a replacement is easily found. Just like customers, employees who feel wanted and valued will want to stay.

It starts at the top. The number-one leader of the organization, the general manager or CEO, must wholeheartedly support a more heart-centered approach to leading the organization by activating the soft skills listed above. This means walking the talk, even when no one is looking, to the point that there are repercussions when a leader behaves in a manner contrary to these principles. It may even mean some changes on the leadership team if certain members don't fully embrace this concept.

Aside from all of this, it's the 'right' thing to do for the world — and for yourself. Research proves that being more compassionate makes you happier, healthier, and live longer.

It is an understanding of these principles that compelled me to write this book. I hope you enjoy it.

1 Chip Conley, *Peak: How Great Companies Get Their Mojo from Maslow* (New Jersey: John Wiley & Sons, 2007).

2 Amy Adkins, *Employee Engagement in U.S. Stagnant in 2015* (Washington, D.C.: Gallup World Headquarters, January 2016).

"If the first button of one's coat is wrongly buttoned, all the rest will be crooked."

GIORDANO BRUNO

SIXTEENTH-CENTURY
ITALIAN DOMINICAN FRIAR,
POET, PHILOSOPHER

– 1 –
LEADERSHIP IN ACTION

For over six years, the hotel had struggled with performance. Cash-strapped ownership, a lengthy economic recession, a secondary location, and dated decor all combined to make it very difficult to achieve financial expectations, and even market share, against better located and updated competitors. Attracting top-notch talent to this environment was a challenge requiring a general manager with a vision of how to 'right the ship,' convince ownership to finance the much-needed renovation, and build a supportive team to make it happen.

The first general manager to arrive on the scene (we'll call him Richard) seemed to be the ideal candidate, as he attended meetings around the hotel and graciously interacted with all the staff members. He spent time getting to know his team and key influencers, as well as the owners. He spent long hours at the hotel and was able to explain what was going on, from the large and tired physical plant to the weekly owner calls to explain the profit and loss statement (in this case mostly loss). While he was an empathetic leader who knew his team, the focus was always on the financial performance, and he always had an excuse for why something couldn't be done.

But the hotel needed more than gracious hospitality. The culture that developed under Richard's leadership was one of conflict avoidance. When the owners asked for something, whether it was an overambitious budget or a barrage of reports, Richard responded by providing whatever they wanted, never explaining why their request was unrealistic or that the same report already existed in a different form. This all distracted the leaders from the real purpose of the hotel — taking care of the guests and employees. This culture of avoidance quickly evolved to a lack of trust as employees realized that Richard was more interested in appeasing everyone than in sticking to the vision and standing up for what was right, even if it meant having uncomfortable conversations.

The hotel needed a senior leader who would appropriately challenge ownership to back off in their demands for short-term performance results and support a longer-term vision that would in time improve the bottom line. It needed a general manager who could rally the executive team with a vision for improved performance and eliminate negative chatter; one who would, when necessary, dismiss executives who didn't get onboard.

It needed someone who would communicate regularly with the staff to ensure that each person understood and embraced the vision and who was relentless in staying true to that vision, even if it meant a step backward in the already downward spiral of financial performance. It needed a leader who had an unrelenting passion for the hotel and the employees. It needed a general manager with courage of conviction — integrity to stand behind the 'right' direction for all.

NEW SHERIFF IN TOWN

Richard couldn't handle the tough conversations required for this situation and was replaced by a new general manager, whom we'll call Tyler.

Within one month of Tyler's arrival, a new sense of strong leadership was apparent as soon as you put a foot in the lobby. Employees moved faster, walked taller, and wore a smile, while in the past they had walked as if the world weighed heavily on their shoulders. They had previously looked as if there would never be a reprieve from the downward spiral that affected their bonuses, number of hours worked, and even whether they continued to have jobs. This insecurity meant that despite being long-term employees, they might be forced to find new jobs, a difficult prospect during an economic recession. Under Tyler's leadership, trust and integrity were restored.

In addition to diving into issues and hitting conflict head-on, Tyler turned the hotel around with increased employee-engagement scores and higher financial performance. He did this by first gaining credibility with the staff and developing a core message of the new direction and vision with easy-to-remember points that were reviewed regularly. This message was broken down further into tangible, achievable

> **Leadership is not just about being Mr. Nice Guy**
>
> Activating soft skills doesn't mean a leader won't discipline an employee or is always 'nice.' Sometimes a situation requires a leader be firm and perhaps even 'not nice.' A leader's role sometimes means making difficult decisions that may be unpopular. Employees might even question if it is the right decision and temporarily impede productivity. While feedback is important and great leaders admit when they make a mistake, if the decision and direction are right for the organization, employees who embrace the direction are the ones you want to have, and the rest are welcome to decide if it's not for them.
>
> The worst scenario is to do nothing for fear of not being liked. Good employees will come around (even if it takes them some time to accept the changes). Similarly, if an employee is causing disruption within the organization, doing nothing will have the rest of the employees feeling a lack of fairness, and distrust and fear will set in.
>
> The bottom line is it's often lonely at the top, but a leader's role is to lead, not to be popular.

goals (both short-term and long-term) for the executive team that reported to him. Everyone knew the direction, how they were going to get there, and what each person's role was in the future success of the hotel.

Tyler communicated regularly to everyone, in clear and concise language, where they were in achieving the goal. Success stories were shared, and the employees involved were recognized. Setbacks were shared too. Even Tyler was not without accountability, as he regularly reviewed what he had accomplished and where he had fallen short with the executive team. His transparency increased the level of trust across the organization.

> "Solidify the team that works with you. Determine who is with you and who is against you and make the necessary decisions on a timely basis (don't procrastinate on the tough decisions of moving out an employee who is not open to the new vision); however, do so with empathy and compassion. It is the task of the senior leader to use the strength of each person as a building block for joint performance."[1]

Tyler got things done by developing a relationship with each employee and understanding what motivated them. They worked hard together and had fun together.

Tough conversations were handled quickly and fairly. If the mission or vision was being compromised, there was a discussion, and loyalty to the hotel and the vision became a condition of employment. Some people didn't buy into the new direction, and in some cases, long-term employees left since they couldn't accept or fit into the new culture.

When positions did become available, Tyler hired the best people he could find. In some cases, positions were open for a few months, as it was difficult to find the right person to fit the new environment. Eventually, however, potential candidates got wind of the change at the hotel (and that it was now a great place to work), and open positions were filled quickly and easily with people who wanted to work for this inspirational GM. Over time, Tyler created the 'dream team' that became unstoppable at accomplishing the mission.

EMBRACING CONFLICT

But that's not to suggest the team agreed all the time. In fact, there were times when the executive meetings were quite heated. When the team left the meeting, however, everyone was aligned and back on message. Tyler fought for his team, and they knew that when confronted by ownership or corporate office, he would stand up for them. Loyalty was key.

Strong leaders get things done. They are passionate and committed to the vision. They fix things, even if it means revamping the process. They are the

> At Southwest Airlines, challenging, debating and facing conflict is an internal culture that is embraced and in fact, employees are trained on how to do this in a respectful and forthright manner. It ensures actions and decisions are well thought out and withstand the rigor of employees seeing them as good decisions or well thought through actions. This approach challenges someone's integrity and causes them to step back and have courage in their convictions.[2]

leaders' employees want to work with because they inspire. They provide clear expectations to members of their team and fight for them behind the scenes. When faced with making a decision, they ask for input and ideas from their team, but ultimately when a decision is made, they are accountable for its implementation and results. The worst situation is no decision at all, where employees are left dangling, not knowing what to do.

WHAT IS THE IMPACT OF INTEGRITY — OR LACK OF IT — IN A HOTEL?

Integrity is doing the right thing even if it might mean losing a guest. When a guest is out of line and verbally, sexually, or physically harassing an employee, leaders must step in and act quickly and efficiently to deal with the situation. When encountering a difficult guest, employees need to feel and see their leaders standing behind them with the same measurement that is expected in reverse.

Lack of integrity can deteriorate into dishonesty.

There's a great deal of temptation in a hotel. Many people, including senior leaders, are around a lot of cash, and that cash comes into the building in many ways. Whether it's advance deposits for an event, cash payments for restaurant and bar tabs, or even some guests paying cash for their accommodation, there are many opportunities for employees to steal.

One hotel had a succession of general managers who, for one reason or another, had their hands in the cookie jar. For the most part, no one knew anything about it, but the hotel could never get on track. It struggled to achieve market share and budget and to keep staff. There were a lot of excuses, but despite hard work and well-intentioned people, the hotel just didn't perform.

Finally, the third general manager was fired, and a new leader arrived, clearly announcing to all employees that stealing, whether it was large amounts of cash or a bottle of wine, would no longer be tolerated. It was as if a veil of darkness and deceit was lifted, and the staff rallied behind the new general manager.

It was tough. A number of employees lost their jobs because they had turned a blind eye to the activity, which meant they were complicit. But less time was spent on covering up wrongdoing and gossiping about it, so employees could spend their time doing productive work. For the first time in many years, the hotel began to achieve performance expectations and became the market leader in RevPAR.

This is integrity in action — making tough decisions because it is the right thing to do and having the courage to face the consequences.

It all starts at the top. Leaders must deal with issues head-on, including those that involve conflict. They must act with integrity even when it seems as if no one is looking. In fact, people are watching, and sometimes rather than speak up and potentially rock the boat, they just leave. Or worse, they say nothing and remain.

HOW ARE YOUR LEADERSHIP SKILLS?

To find out how you score on the leadership scale, take the following Leadership Quiz.

Identify one of your leaders and respond to the following questions with this person in mind. Rate their adoption of these skills on a scale of 1 to 5, where 1 is non-existent and 5 is above and beyond others in a similar role. When several questions are posed around a particular topic, rate it based on the overall sense of the topic.

1. Does this leader have a *vision* for their department or area as well as a plan to execute it?
   1 2 3 4 5

2. In a *crisis*, does this leader respond with calm and clear direction? Do people naturally gravitate to them for guidance and reassurance?
   1 2 3 4 5

3. Does this leader provide ongoing, consistent, and clear *communication* about the vision as well as what is happening within and around the organization?
   1 2 3 4 5

4. Does this leader *give advice* clearly and concisely so that people don't waste time and energy doing unnecessary work?
   1 2 3 4 5

5. Are their deadlines managed effectively with *advance planning*, follow-up, and coordinated effort, thus avoiding a mad dash at the end that upsets the organization?
   1 2 3 4 5

6. Does this leader ensure there is **accountability** with each of their direct reports and/or task responsibilities?
   1 2 3 4 5

7. How does this leader handle **decision-making**? Do they delay it or avoid it completely? Are they too quick to make a decision without all the information? Or, are they able to effectively communicate how and why the decision was made and stand behind it when challenged?
   1 2 3 4 5

8. Do they **'manage by walking around'** to find out what is happening, or do they stick to their office and very rarely come out to see how the team is doing and if they need help?
   1 2 3 4 5

9. Does this leader handle **difficult conversation**s with kindness, compassion, and a caring approach as quickly as possible, or do they avoid the issue and sometimes even pretend it doesn't exist?
   1 2 3 4 5

10. Do they **empower employees** to make decisions, even if that means a mistake might be made, and use those mistakes as coaching opportunities?
    1 2 3 4 5

11. Does this leader **motivate** the team with positive guidance and direction, especially in challenging times?
    1 2 3 4 5

12. How often does this leader give public **recognition** when an employee goes above and beyond what is expected, including giving positive reinforcement whenever it is merited?
    1 2 3 4 5

13. Is this leader **authentic**? Do they admit mistakes and share success and failure stories so that all can learn from them? Would their team consider them to be transparent?
    1 2 3 4 5

14. Does this leader **uphold the company's values** and decisions made by the organization? Do they roll up their sleeves when necessary, especially when the team is under a deadline?
    1 2 3 4 5

15. Do they **ask for input** and ideas from their team, or do they dictate how things should be done without involving those people who actually 'do' the work?
    1 2 3 4 5

16. How effective is this leader at **listening** to employees? Do they ask clarifying questions as well as probe to make sure they really understand what the employee is saying?
    1 2 3 4 5

17. Is this leader **empathetic** to employees, first understanding what is happening in their lives and then 'walking in their shoes'? Do they help when necessary, even if it means rolling up their own sleeves?
    1 2 3 4 5

18. Do they provide **feedback** in a constructive, fair way and on a consistent basis (not just at performance-review time)? Do they give feedback in a private setting?
    1 2 3 4 5

19. Do they wear a smile and consistently come to work with a **positive attitude**?
    1 2 3 4 5

20. Is there an **esprit de corps** in this department? Do they have fun together and genuinely want to be there?
    1 2 3 4 5

21. In the department or area they lead, is the **employee turnover** at an acceptable level or is there an unusually high number of people vacating their positions? How difficult is it to recruit for vacant positions within their department or area? Are positions open for a long time?
    1 2 3 4 5

22. How many people have been promoted under this leader? If a new leader, have they identified top talent and developed a plan to motivate and keep them? Does this leader **develop their team** and prepare their people for the next step, whether that is a lateral move, promotion, or even as their own replacement?
    1 2 3 4 5

23. How **engaged** are their teams? What is the engagement score? If it is not measured, do their people demonstrate the commitment to excellence and pride in their work that differentiates great teams from average ones?
    1 2 3 4 5

24. Within their department or area, are the ***employee satisfaction scores*** at an acceptable level? If there isn't an employee satisfaction survey, do employees appear to have fun and generally like being there?
1 2 3 4 5

25. Does this leader achieve the ***financial results*** expected of their department or area?
1 2 3 4 5

Total Score _____

SCORING

100 to 125   This leader is a rock star — do everything you can to keep this person on your team!

75 to 99   This leader is doing well; however, some behavioral adjustments could have a dramatic impact.

50 to 74   The behavior of this leader is a concern, requiring an objective view and coaching to get them on track to be effective in their role.

49 or less   The organization is heading for challenging times, and it is time to either develop a plan to improve leadership skills with coaching and training or change the leaders.

Now that you've completed the questionnaire for someone else, do it again considering your own leadership skills. A look in the mirror never hurts!

1   Peter F. Drucker, *The Effective Executive: The Definite Guide to Getting the Right Things Done* (New York: Harper Business, 1966).

2   Joanna S. Lublin, "The High Cost of Avoiding Conflict at Work," *Wall Street Journal*, accessed May 3, 2018, www.wsj.com/articles/the-high-cost-of-avoiding-conflict-at-work-1392390289.

> *"Leadership is lifting a person's vision to high sights, the raising of a person's performance to a higher standard, the building of a personality beyond its normal limitations."*
>
> PETER DRUCKER

– 2 –

WHAT MAKES A GREAT HOTEL LEADER?

There are thousands of books on leadership. Given that there is already so much information available, why do authors continue to write on the topic, and why do so many people continue to complain about their bosses? Historically, hotel leaders were measured predominantly on financial performance and, to a lesser degree, on guest satisfaction. In recent years, this metric has shifted toward employee engagement as having equal and possibly greater importance than guest satisfaction.

This shift is due in part to the recognition that satisfied employees are more productive and will provide better service to guests. Engaged employees will communicate issues to their supervisors more readily, respond faster to guest requests, and generally get along better with their fellow employee. When mistakes do happen, engaged employees tend to accept responsibility faster, often avoiding wasted time figuring out 'who did it,' and use the time to resolve the issue so it won't happen again.

This is as true in a hotel as in any other workplace.

Years ago, a hotel general manager would line up staff to check to see if their nails were clean and bark out their orders for the day. That same general manager would then turn to a guest and suddenly become gracious and accommodating.

Becoming a different person depending on whom you are speaking to is known as the Jekyll and Hyde syndrome, and it doesn't make for a happy workplace. The problem can be eliminated through behavior that is consistent, whether interacting with guest or employee.

> **Leadership**
>
> A note here about terminology. Throughout the book, I use the terms "leadership" and "leaders" in the specific context of hotels. When I use these terms, I'm referring to anyone who has people reporting to them, whether they are a front office manager, a housekeeping supervisor, or a general manager. They are responsible for effectively delegating work and resources to get things done, including taking care of the guests and the employees within their area.

This change often requires leaders to learn and practice new skills, to have employees work more collaboratively and still get the work done.

This might seem daunting for some leaders who believe the way to manage is to give specific direction and possibly even exact instructions on how to do something. Some leaders feel they need to have distance from their teams and not show their human side, especially when admitting they have made a mistake. If that is your management style, the more authentic approach that this book suggests will feel quite foreign and you may be skeptical about it — I encourage you to read on.

It doesn't need to be an overnight transformation, but small steps in the direction of leading with your heart and using soft skills will bring great rewards. I have seen a wide variety of leadership approaches in my consulting practice and, without fail, those leaders who adopted a heart-centric approach, consistent with both employees and guests, were the ones with the highest-performing areas, whether a department or the entire hotel.

LEADING WITH THE HEART

Leading with your heart means treating people in a caring way so that everyone is recognized for who they are and has a feeling of belonging. It means activating soft skills such as empathy, compassion, graciousness, trust, respect, and integrity.

This is really tested during times of stress — a dissatisfied guest voicing displeasure, employees who have worked double shifts with not enough time to rest and re-energize, or even financial pressure because the hotel is not performing. It's at times like these that leaders must overcome the tendency to forget to treat others in a kind, respectful manner, or even to take out their frustrations on other staff members.

Often the level of customer service is really the differentiator between hotels, so if embracing a heart-centric approach will lead to better guest experiences, why not do it? It also has the added financial benefit of lower staff recruitment costs, less overtime to cover gaps in service, and less training costs for new employees.

SERVANT LEADER CONCEPT

"The truly effective and inspiring leaders aren't actually driven to lead people; they are driven to serve them."

SIMON SINEK, A GOOD LEADER SERVES[1]

Robert K. Greenleaf developed the philosophy of servant leadership in 1970. In essence, this perspective turns upside down the way we look at who the most important person in the organization is (the employee) and what this (new) role is for leaders.

It means leaders who help each member of the team to be able to do their job, providing them with all the tools they need to get the tasks accomplished, helping them when mistakes are made, supporting them in discussions with senior management, and focusing on their strengths to bring out the best they can be. This leads to trust, which results in loyalty.

In the hotel world, the concept of service is especially poignant, as leaders already use this approach to deal with guests. Success will come to those who learn to use the same skill with employees. It starts with leaders first identifying skills and abilities an individual employee possesses as well as functions they perform especially well, and helping them to become even better at them. Leaders then recognize them in front of their peers for these abilities and work with them to figure out other ways they can use their unique talents or expand to do other similar functions. The leader thus becomes the servant and a catalyst to uncover hidden talents and abilities.

An example of servant leadership is Cindy's boss. Cindy is a reservations agent who is terrific at developing a relationship with each guest or travel agent who calls in to book a room. While her calls may last longer than any other agent in the hotel, Cindy's conversion rate is well over the industry standard of 31 percent.

The director of reservations acknowledged her ability and set up a special phone number for top travel agents and former guests to call in directly to Cindy, leveraging the relationships she had built up, and book more business. Travel agents couldn't wait to call Cindy and have her personally handle their reservations, and business from these top accounts went up.

HOW TO BE A GREAT LEADER

Let's start with the basics. These may seem self-evident, but their absence in some hotels I've visited leads me to believe they need to be reinforced.

LEADERSHIP BASICS

It all comes down to some pretty fundamental things.

Use the basic courtesies of "Please" and "Thank you" with every interaction. I'm surprised at the lack of use of these two powerful words, whether it's in the checkout line at the grocery store, a customer ordering dinner in at a fine dining room, or a hotel leader speaking to staff. Using them not only makes you more polite, but treating someone else with respect slows you down to become more gracious to yourself and the other people in your life.

Smile often. This is the easiest habit to adopt. A genuine smile acknowledges someone as a person, and it's easy to know if it's genuine because a smile from the heart lights up the whole face.

Greet everyone when you see them. When someone arrives at the office, look up from your work and offer them a genuine "Good morning," ideally with their name and with a smile. As a hiker, I've noticed that when you cross paths with another hiker, the protocol is to smile and say, "Good morning." Why not do this at work?

In Europe, a long tradition of politeness remains today. French shopkeepers have a lovely way of greeting everyone who walks into their shop with a "Bonjour" and saying "Au revoir" when they leave. While conducting a six-month project in Italy, I was delighted to see team members kiss each other hello and goodbye after an absence, even if it was just for a weekend.

Use someone's name often. The most beautiful word in the world is your own name. Get to know each member of your team's name and use it often. Isadore Sharp, founder and chairman of Four Seasons Hotels and Resorts, is famous for remembering more than just names. If he knew something about an employee, such as a spouse being in the hospital, he would ask about them the next time he saw the employee, even if it was six months later.

Make it a habit to use a guest's name at least once in every interaction. At many restaurants, the first thing the server does is to introduce themselves. Using a guest's name immediately starts the emotional bond and makes the service process more personal.

Be respectful. Ask someone to do something for you rather than tell them. Give them the opportunity to reply with alternatives that might be even better options. And speaking of asking, ask for feedback on everything, including how you are doing as a leader.

Make eye contact, especially with those employees who are working on a computer, such as front desk or concierge staff. And speaking of technology, leaders need to disengage from their mobile devices when speaking to an employee or guest.

Now that we have the basics out of the way, let's consider my 10 Keys to GREAT Leadership:

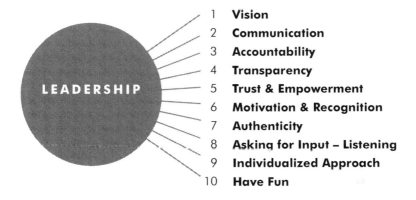

1. **Vision**
2. **Communication**
3. **Accountability**
4. **Transparency**
5. **Trust & Empowerment**
6. **Motivation & Recognition**
7. **Authenticity**
8. **Asking for Input – Listening**
9. **Individualized Approach**
10. **Have Fun**

TEN KEYS TO GREAT LEADERSHIP

1. Have a clear vision

> *"Great leaders are almost always great simplifiers, who can cut through argument, debate and doubt, to offer a solution everybody can understand."*
>
> COLIN POWELL, FORMER UNITED STATES SECRETARY OF STATE AND RETIRED FOUR-STAR GENERAL IN THE UNITED STATES ARMY

The role of visionary in a hotel is sometimes left to the general manager. Too often operational leaders see their responsibility as task-oriented, spending little time thinking about how to improve the process. Every leader needs to have a vision for what is within their area of responsibility — the vision or goal they are looking to achieve.

Being a visionary leader is a logical requirement for general managers and the executive team, but one of the best examples I have seen was a department head. New to her job as room-service manager, Tina wanted to grow revenue within her department by 10 percent. While that may not seem like much, this was a department that had declining revenue, as corporate clients preferred the grab-and-go from the Starbucks in the attached mall and often entertained clients over an evening meal at a hot new restaurant outside the hotel.

Tina determined the challenging goal of 10-percent revenue improvement in the room-service department within one year and came up with a few ideas to get there. But more importantly, she figured out the impact in the tip pool for the order takers and servers. By figuring out the benefit to each team member, she was able to bring them onboard with her plan.

Personal benefits for the people involved were reviewed at the start of the meeting to renew the vision. Then Tina brainstormed with the team on how they were going to accomplish the goal. Room-service tables were old and cumbersome and slowed down delivery. Convincing the food and beverage director to buy new ones was Tina's first step in the implementation, and it showed the team that she had management support.

To help explain the menu better, the staff got to taste each food item, including the daily special, so that they could talk about it with guests more easily. They were encouraged to state the specials with enthusiasm and passion, which was easier once they had tried them.

Each month, they had a special item they promoted. It started with order takers suggesting water with each room-service order. Then it moved to wine and dessert at dinner time.

Front desk and bellmen also got in on the act, talking to guests when they arrived about the terrific room-service menu, including pointing it out when delivering luggage in the guestroom.

Tina achieved her goal of a 10-percent increase in room-service revenue within three months!

2. Communicate effectively

According to *The Globe and Mail*, 59 percent of employees don't know what makes their product different from the competition.[2]

How employees feel about where they work can be directly correlated to what customers think about the brand. It's not only for the big stuff, such as rolling out the business plan for the following year for the hotel or company; it's also the details, such as clearly communicating expectations of each position. People want to know the rules and what is expected of them. This builds loyalty.

3. Foster accountability

Follow up regularly to ensure accountability for each member of the team. This includes you as the leader — if you say you will do something, do it! This builds a foundation of trust.

Throughout North America, the most common attribute employees want to see in the workplace is accountability. In drilling down and identifying what this looks like, we find it is a clear understanding of the expectations outlined by their boss. When the deadline is met, employees want their boss to follow up on the assignment or project and give feedback on how they did.

It also means that everyone is expected to meet deadlines, knowing that when they don't, there will be repercussions. This ensures that everyone is treated fairly and equally. It also means that work isn't held up because one employee is waiting for another employee to do their part.

There is a direct correlation between fairness and engagement. If a leader is seen as unfair, employee engagement will be low. Therefore, give feedback that is fair, consistent, and immediate. When employees aren't a fit, move them out as quickly as possible. Handle the tough conversations with kindness and caring as soon as you have full information. Be honest, especially if someone isn't making it — all the rest of the staff expects you to do something about it.

Accountability to their teams is also expected at the leadership level. Employees should be given realistic deadlines for assignments and not told at the last minute when something is due. Expectations should be clear, concise, and not changed midpoint, and the workload should be distributed evenly.

4. Facilitate and encourage transparency

Even the most top-secret discussions often have leaks. Thus information reaching employees can be incomplete and out of context and can start gossip and misinformation going around the hotel, which distracts everyone from the job at hand. As much as possible, without jeopardizing the confidentiality of guests or employees, share information as quickly as possible.

When decisions affecting employees are made, particularly if they are controversial, information needs to be communicated clearly, providing the background for why the decision was made. If a leader doesn't feel free to communicate information effectively, they need to consider if this organization is consistent with their values and possibly consider leaving for another position.

Transparency also means that leaders are the same person with a guest as with an employee. A friend of mine called it having one life. It takes a lot of work to change your attitude and in some cases personality depending on who you are with. Inevitably, employees see through it, and the only person you are fooling is yourself. Consistency and transparency are a lot easier and less stressful.

5. Trust and empower employees

Guests around the world trust hoteliers with their safety, their well-being, and their possessions. Guests trust housekeepers to resist the temptation around them whenever they enter a guest room. Celebrities trust that the hotel staff won't divulge to fans or the press where they are staying, and in some cases their idiosyncrasies.

The trust of guests is implicit in a hotel. Trust must also be implicit in employees. Such trust starts with leaders developing a culture in which employees feel safe not just in the physical sense, but also safe in speaking up, identifying problems, and offering solutions.

Trust and empowerment go hand-in-hand. At every Ritz-Carlton Hotel, each employee is empowered to solve a guest problem on their own without escalating the situation to a superior for a decision. This empowerment is backed up with the ability to use up to $2,000 at their discretion to solve the problem. It could be a rebate to a complaining guest at the front desk or in the restaurant, or paying for a taxi to deliver a forgotten briefcase. This is one of the reasons that Ritz-Carlton Hotel Company has won the Malcolm Baldridge award twice for providing outstanding service delivery, the only hotel company to receive this recognition.

6. Motivate employees and recognize their achievements

Serving guests can be a difficult job. Often, it's not physical strength that's required to get the job done, but emotional and physiological strength to do the repetitive, tedious, or challenging tasks needed when working the 'back of the house.'

Motivating employees based on what is important to them is an empathetic and compassionate approach to leading effectively. Get to know each person on the team for who they are as individuals. Build a relationship with each person based on what makes them tick and their personal values. Once you know this, practice empathy, which we will discuss in more depth in Chapter 4.

As much as possible, recognize and reward behavior that exemplifies the organization's values and culture. Be specific when acknowledging actions and work well done.

7. Walk the talk — authenticity

Be human — share your stories, successes, and failures. Admit when you make a mistake. This shows integrity, and the team will watch the leader's actions even more than they listen to what is said. Know yourself — your strengths and weaknesses and, most importantly, what you value. What do you value, and do your actions and behaviors exemplify what you believe?

Walk the talk — live the example and uphold the values of the organization and its culture. Roll up your sleeves when necessary, especially when the team is under deadline.

8. Ask for input, and then listen

Ask for input, ideas, and solutions. Gather all the information possible when making a decision, including asking employees for their ideas and solutions.

Listen — really listen. Give your full attention and ask questions to make sure you have a clear understanding of what everyone is trying to say. Be gracious.

> A *Harvard Business Review* article states that listening with empathy is a learnable skill involving the following three behaviors on the part of the leader or listener:
>
> 1. Watch for nonverbal cues like body language, facial movements, and voice tonality. Factor in all the senses, not just hearing.
>
> 2. Recite back what has been heard or summarize the key points to make sure the meaning is understood, and acknowledge that the listener is processing the information.
>
> 3. Respond with questions that either qualify or clarify what has been said. This also keeps the communication going.[3]

9. One size doesn't fit all — a customized approach to leading

Serving your team to bring out the best in them means your role as a leader is flexible and agile, which requires you to adjust your approach and style to each team member depending on the person or situation. The leader serves as a conduit to achieve the best performance each member is able to bring to their role, based on their abilities and unique strengths.

I recently worked on a project with a hotel sales and marketing division. Two senior team members were each assigned a quarterly stretch goal to exceed budget. One person wanted just three pieces of information: the expectation for the end result, the budget available to accomplish it, and the time frame to get it completed. Beyond this, the team member wanted management to leave them on their own. Each day, pleasantries were exchanged and a bi-weekly one-on-one was held to update on the status of the project. However, at no time did they ask for help or even input on how they approached something.

The second employee, of equal tenure in their position, had the same goal. However, every day they stopped by to discuss one question or another, get feedback on their progress, and looked forward to weekly one-on-ones to make sure they were on the right track.

Neither of these approaches is right or wrong, but they are different based on the personality and abilities of the salesperson, and they require different types of leadership.

The leader's role is to figure out which approach works best for each employee, including to what degree they want or need interaction and what motivates them, and give them what they need even if it's unexpressed. Leaders who can calibrate their interactions with each team member and situation will unleash hidden potential in their people.

10. Have fun!

Having a sense of humor and using it liberally is a valuable skill for a leader. It can defuse a hostile situation and make the workday move along faster and more easily. Create an environment of camaraderie, espirit de corps, and trust. If the team is open to it, do things outside of work together; if they prefer to go home to their families after work, set aside some time within work hours to spend time as a team, having fun.

If you're not having fun, your team won't either — and given all of the hours that are required to run a hotel, isn't it worth the effort?

Leading a hotel is like conducting a symphony orchestra. The conductor may not look as if he's doing much, but he establishes a clear vision of what he wants. Will the music be fast or slow? Will the predominant sounds come from the woodwinds or the brass section? What impact will more percussion have on the overall sound?

Will the hotel be known for its friendly service? Will people come from miles around to dine in the restaurant? Will there be a cookie jar or crisp apple on the front desk? What impact will a bellman remembering a guest's name have on the overall experience?

While each musician follows the music specifically written for their instrument and its part, they regularly glance at the conductor to make sure they are following his lead. When someone doesn't follow instructions given in rehearsal, the conductor ensures accountability and provides the needed attention to fix the problem. At the same time, he praises individuals for extraordinary performance and does everything possible to help them to shine.

Likewise, even knowledgeable hotel staff will always be mindful of the leader's requirements, and an effective one knows when to give extra coaching to individuals whose performance has gone a bit flat.

Finally, the orchestra takes its collective bow, and the conductor pays special tribute to those musicians who gave an especially fine performance.

The heart-centric hotel leader does the same thing, praising staff for pulling off a particularly challenging event or keeping the hotel running smoothly through an emergency.

The number-one reason people leave their jobs is an ineffective boss. If you learn, practice, and live the ten skills described above, you will be a great hotel leader. You will attract great employees, raise each individual's performance to even higher levels than they could have imagined, resulting in more engaged teams and customers and, ultimately, dramatic increases in financial success.

1 Simon Sinek, "A Good Leader Serves," accessed May 3, 2108, www.askmen.com/money/career_300/349_simon-sinek-a-good-leader-serves.html.

2 Kim Benedict, "Employee retention is not just about pizza lunches and parties," *Globe & Mail*, March 25, 2017.

3 Christine M. Riordan, "Three Ways Leaders Can Listen with More Empathy," *Harvard Business Review*, accessed December 19, 2014, https://hbr.org/2014/01/three-ways-leaders-can-listen-with-more-empathy.

> "What is a lobby boy?
> A lobby boy is completely invisible, yet always in sight. A lobby boy remembers what people hate. A lobby boy anticipates the client's needs before the needs are needed. A lobby boy is, above all, discreet to a fault. Our guests know that their deepest secrets, some of which are frankly rather unseemly, will go with us to our graves. So keep your mouth shut, Zero."
>
> THE GRAND BUDAPEST HOTEL
> ORIGINAL SCREENPLAY:
> WES ANDERSON & HUGO GUINNESS[1]

– 3 –

WHAT IS GREAT SERVICE?

Have you ever walked into a hotel and immediately felt relaxed, comfortable, and at home? The staff acknowledged you and smiled at you. Regardless of the style, the décor was comfortable, inviting you to sit down and stay awhile. The lighting was bright enough to read the newspaper, yet still subdued enough to feel like your home rather than a commercial enterprise. Even the air smelled fresh. Every detail had been carefully crafted and maintained to provide a warm welcome.

But feeling at home is more than all of that. To truly feel at home, you must trust that during each step of your lodging journey, you will be safe and comfortable and feel you are the most important person there. Employees must be responsive, handling your every request efficiently and effortlessly, no matter how busy they are, even if there is a crisis going on elsewhere.

Just like Zero, the lobby boy in *The Grand Budapest Hotel*, staff must be trained and educated to create this feeling for guests. Such training and education is the mark of great hotel leadership.

Today, the bar on service in the hotel world is being raised ever higher. Hotels that provide unique customer experiences and leave positive, long-lasting memories are the ones that are poised to exceed their market share, dramatically improve revenue, and beat the competition. This means leaders must up their game too, and it may challenge some leaders outside the comfort zone of just dealing with the technical side of their jobs. If they ignore this challenge, they risk failure in moving up the ranks.

The foundation for these amazing experiences and memories, however, is genuine hospitality, so let's start by defining exactly what hospitality is all about.

GRACIOUS HOSPITALITY IS NOT NEW

Providing a place for weary travelers to stay for the night dates back to Joseph and Mary. After all, "No room at the inn" is just another way of saying "No vacancy."

But what is hospitality, really? Merriam-Webster defines it simply as "generous and friendly treatment of visitors and guests." In her study *Hospitality in Early Modern England*, though, Felicity Heal takes a more philosophical perspective, saying that hospitality transforms strangers into friends and friends into family.[2]

According to Heal, seventeenth-century British innkeeping had three principles:

1. Authentic relationship between host and guest from the heart,
2. Hosts who understood and respected the guest's background and preferences as well as cultural biases,
3. Selfless concern for wellbeing of others, freely given.

Sound familiar? These three-hundred-year-old principles are the same ones we purport to provide today in the hospitality industry.

Today, we talk about providing experiences that are authentic and personalized, enabling hotels to stand out from their competitors. This requires that service providers give something of themselves versus doing it by a book of standards that can become rote. When they do it right, there is a connection between the employee and the guest that makes the experience magical. Those hotels where the general manager and other employees talk to guests, spending time with them, are usually the ones that garner the best comments on TripAdvisor.

Learning something about the guest's preferences, interests, and purpose of their visit — either prior to arrival or during their stay — allows us to provide new services based on customer needs. The family staying for the weekend with young children, for example, gets babysitting services; the business traveler can order dinner from room service while en route from the airport; the conference attendee can squeeze in a visit to an important historical site with a knowledgeable guide. Responding to these types of requests quickly and smoothly exemplifies great service and is all in a day's work for a good host.

A SANCTUARY OF DISCRETION

Discretion is an important issue in hotels, especially for those that host royalty, celebrities, and dignitaries. While they typically travel under an alias (I learned some very creative names while handling the world tours for top rock 'n' roll bands and singers), it's very tempting for employees to secretly share with the press who is staying in the hotel and tidbits curious fans would find interesting. Hotels must remain a sanctuary of discretion.

This same privacy must also hold for employees. Leaders have an important role in maintaining this bond of secrecy.

There has been a lot of attention recently on hotel safety. Recent events, from the bombing at the Taj Hotel in Mumbai to the Las Vegas shooting from the thirty-second floor at Mandalay Bay Hotel in Las Vegas, have made hotel security staff much more aware of each person who enters the building.

Leaders play a major role in keeping their staff and guests safe in times of crisis. They need to increase their awareness of potential trouble. This starts with the general manager and other leaders interacting with guests, especially suspicious people who walk in the door. This has the additional benefit that employees see leaders having more interactions with guests regularly and not just at times of crisis. These interactions also provide opportunities for leaders to coach the staff in the same level of awareness they have themselves.

Hospitality is a noble profession and, at least to some degree, a respected one. Every year, large numbers of newly minted graduates aspire to move through the ranks in a hotel to the pinnacle position of general manager. Almost every one of those positions requires more than just skill. It requires a genuine desire to build an emotional connection with every single guest and a commitment to provide selfless service, which is really another way of describing the servant attitude I talked about earlier. This quality is rare and worthy of acknowledgment, recognition, and respect.

How you develop the ability to have an emotional connection and provide selfless service is by putting aside your own needs and issues and walking in the guest's shoes. To do that, you have to ask a few questions to understand what is happening in their lives right now. Too often we fall into the trap of thinking we can figure out what is going on in someone's life based on what they look like. But a person's outward appearance can be a façade and not a reflection of what is really going on. Asking the right questions and activating empathy will help achieve these rare skills of connection and selfless service. I will discuss this in more detail in Chapter 4.

Is it possible that, in some cases, the twenty-first-century hospitality profession has strayed from these aspirations?

I believe it has, and that bringing them back will require staff who personify this attitude. Management must learn to recognize these people during the hiring process. Then, having hired the right team for their attitude, they must provide training that will develop knowledge and practice to allow them to provide selfless service for every guest, based on individual need. Only then will the profession return to the fundamentals of true hospitality.

I have experienced this type of service outside the hospitality industry, at my local vegetable market, where the employees have developed an emotional connection with customers that is priceless. One day I watched a particular employee interact with other customers. Often, he knew their names (and they his) and he looked them in the eye when he spoke to them, creating the impression that he was giving them inside information that others wouldn't be privy to.

Whenever I walk in, they make me feel special. Perhaps that's why the store is always bustling despite prices that are sometimes double those of their competitors, and why they are currently expanding to double the square footage.

This quality of service works for a vegetable store, and it works for a hotel.

WHAT IS GREAT SERVICE, ANYWAY?

In speaking with hotel general managers and sales teams around the world, I often ask what differentiates them from their competitors. Invariably, the answer comes back, "It's our service." This answer comes regardless of the hotel's star rating by Forbes Travel Guide or diamond rating by AAA. It's very difficult to measure service and on its own, without a deeper explanation, is not a very helpful differentiating factor.

Great leaders don't rely on service just happening. They map out possible scenarios their team could encounter and options for how they could respond. This training method helps employees understand that their creativity and insights are needed as well, not just in the practice sessions but while on the floor, dealing with each guest interaction.

Providing great service means adapting to suit the circumstances. That was my experience when I dined twice in one week at the prestigious French Laundry in Yountville, California.

THE FRENCH LAUNDRY EXPERIENCE

My first experience was an intimate dinner for two, where we not only savored every bite but doubled our enjoyment by talking about it together.

Our focus was on the food and the overall gourmet experience, and we couldn't help noticing the orchestration of the staff so that each employee performed a finely tuned role. The server was able to 'read' us correctly and understand that we wanted a more detailed description of the food and wine, which he then provided. This engagement between the staff and us, while discreet and reserved, was much appreciated.

Our second visit happened a few days later when a friend asked us to fill in for a couple of cancellations at her ten-person dinner party.

With wine and conversation flowing among ten opinionated and interesting people, the service staff required a different sort of calibration. They navigated expertly around the conversation and did not describe the food unless someone asked. Again, they were able to read the needs of their guests and act accordingly.

In both cases, the service appeared to just happen. That's because the staff were professionals who understood their role and adjusted the amount of information they gave about the food depending on the circumstances. They were discreet and modified their involvement with the guests depending on what their intuition told them.

I lost count of the number of staff members servicing our table, even when it was just for two people. This is another measure of an extraordinary service experience, as it allows time for an employee to go beyond doing the technical side of their job — in this case, delivering a plate of food — and take a moment to determine if there is something else the guest might need and then provide it quickly and efficiently.

This amazing service didn't happen in a vacuum. Thomas Keller, owner and chef, made sure that he hired the right team to lead each aspect of the dinner journey and trained them well to bring this result. He is a hands-on chef and leads by example so that his staff attains his high standards.

It's not surprising that The French Laundry has been listed as one of the top restaurants in the US for many years. It is located in a nondescript little house with a beige interior and no pictures on the walls. The staff members are dressed in neutral beige and white. All the linens and china are white. This 'plain' environment is consistent with The French Laundry brand, which is to ensure there is no distraction from the food. It's a wonderful experience and well worth the $295 per person (at time of writing) for the prix fixe menu. I would encourage you to try it once in your life — and if you are offered a seat a few nights later, say "Yes!"

Bottom line, great service is impossible to measure or even define, but I've developed five fundamentals for hotel leaders to begin the journey:

1. Hire the right people — people who not only have the technical skills to do whatever is required in the job but also the attitude of selfless service. Even more important, hire candidates who have the ability to use empathy, since that is what anticipating customer needs is about.

2. Provide regular, ongoing, relentless training for all employees to keep skills fresh and activated. Even training unrelated to the job function keeps employees engaged and shows that management really values and cares about them.

3. Implement a staffing model that ensures there are enough people to be available and ready whenever a guest needs something. This gives employees time to offer extra service when the opportunity arises.
4. Establish an employee-recognition program that supports the attitude and behaviors you want to be repeated and partner it with rewarding extraordinary acts of service that go above and beyond what is expected.
5. An often overlooked requirement of leaders is to develop and promote their team to become future great leaders. This means assessing employees with a future role in mind and determining the necessary skills or abilities they need to build to get there.

The benefit of a luxury environment is that there are more staff, which means they can spend more time with each guest in the knowledge that other duties are automatically being taken up by other employees.

However, great service needn't be restricted to luxury hotels. With staff who are friendly and welcoming, who smile and take a genuine interest, who listen to guests and respond appropriately, every hotel can provide a level of service that reflects the true meaning of hospitality.

A luxurious physical product is not enough to create guest engagement. The essential element is an emotional connection between the employees and guests. It is this indication of humanity that increases spending and long-term loyalty. Throughout this book, we will explore ways to increase guest engagement, and particularly how leaders can contribute to its development.

Leaders should be invisible to guests, but their presence always felt by staff. Who knows, maybe Zero at the Grand Budapest Hotel was a budding leader, as his mentor's quote at the begin of this chapter is really a mantra for leaders. Let's exchange "leader" for "lobby boy" and "employee" for "customer":

"What is a leader? A leader is completely invisible, yet always in sight. A leader remembers what employees hate. A leader anticipates the employee's needs before the needs are needed. A leader is, above all, discreet to a fault. Our employees know that their deepest secrets, some of which are frankly rather unseemly, will go with us to our graves. So keep your mouth shut, Zero."

1 Wes Anderson and Hugo Guinness, *The Grand Budapest Hotel*. Film. Directed by Wes Anderson. Fox Searchlight Pictures, March 7, 2014.

2 F. Heal, *Hospitality in Early Modern England* (Oxford: Clarendon Press, 1990).

"Empathy is the cornerstone of extraordinary customer service."

JO-ANNE HILL

– 4 –

EMPATHY AND CUSTOMER SERVICE

In 1978 the airline industry in the US was deregulated, which produced a domino effect on the travel and hospitality industries. Deregulation meant lower airfare, which allowed more and more people from wider demographics to travel, a trend that continued into the dawn of the '80s and beyond.

This shift coincided with a dramatic increase in hotel supply, and the industry naturally succumbed to the law of supply and demand. Of course, as hotel supply began to increase, guests had more and more choice available.

The third element that had a dramatic impact on the hospitality industry was the 'all about me' mentality of the '80s, this saw a rise in self-centeredness and selfishness, and this often came at the expense of focusing on the needs of others. It marked a decline in empathy.

Perhaps not surprisingly, this new era saw the beginning of higher demands from guests, who were prepared to pay more but wanted more in return. This often included being recognized for who they are. Hotel service became more refined, with great attention to the smallest of details and more personalization of guests' stay, whether it was for one night or ten.

In response to these shifts, the hospitality community coined the term "anticipating guests' needs" and then went further to state that this included unexpressed needs. In some cases, it means anticipating the need even before the guest recognizes it. For service providers to be able to provide that level of service, to truly step into a guest's shoes, they must practice and apply the skill of empathy.

Great hotel leaders recognized that their world had just changed. Employees couldn't be expected to suddenly become more hospitable and empathetic all by themselves without training, coaching, and modeling by their leaders. Leaders realized they needed to respond, especially in areas such as the front desk, where guests often have their first and last interaction with the hotel. It's also where guests typically end up seeking resolution of issues and follow-up.

Empathy and Customer Service // 45

Some leaders got it; others didn't. The hallmark of a great leader is being able to finesse difficult situations — such as guests who have overindulged at the bar and become abusive to employees, or a rowdy party at the pool that impacts other guests — so that all guests are satisfied with the outcome.

As Roman Krznaric pointed out in his book *Empathy: Why it Matters and How to Get It*, empathy is imagining you are in the other person's shoes, figuring out what they are feeling, and determining a course of action that will acknowledge, improve, or potentially even resolve a given situation.[1] All of this in a matter of seconds.

Imagine you are a guest who just arrived at the front desk late at night after the airline lost your luggage. What are all the emotions you might be feeling, especially if you have a career-altering presentation the next day and no change of clothing? Add to the mix possible jetlag and sleep deprivation and a dead cell phone.

Acknowledging how horrible it must be to have this happen, an empathetic and well-trained front desk employee could offer to follow up with the airline to try to have the bags delivered faster. Going further, they might provide an overnight amenity kit with a toothbrush and other necessities, or even after-hours access to a store to replace missing clothing. While this doesn't solve the situation of the missing suitcase — only the airline can do that — it does acknowledge and improve the situation for the guest.

> *"You never really understand a person until you consider things from his point of view... Until you climb inside of his skin and walk around in it."*
>
> HARPER LEE, *TO KILL A MOCKINGBIRD*

If they are to provide this level of service, employees need to be empathetic to guests, and that is why empathy is the cornerstone of great service. Without it, it's unlikely that you can have great service. If hotel staff are unable to tap into and understand how a guest is feeling and respond accordingly, it's unlikely that their behavior will match what is required. Interestingly, empathetic service doesn't need to cost much: a comforting smile after a difficult transfer from the airport, or chamomile tea delivered when someone mentions they have a cold.

The Dorchester hotel in London has 336 guest rooms with eight hundred well-trained, well-cared-for employees. Senior leaders, right up to the general manager, make a point of getting to know each employee, not just their name but also something about them. Leaders treat employees with respect and a sense of dignity, just like it's expected they treat each and every guest. And it works. Whenever you meet an employee in the hallway, they always stop, acknowledge you, and smile, and if they happen to know your name they will use it. Whatever service they are delivering, they always do it with a smile, and when asked to do something extra they do so graciously.

During a recent stay there, I ordered dinner from room service. After the food arrived, I asked if I could have a kettle to make tea, as I was staying for several nights. "Certainly, no problem at all," was the answer. As the employee handed me the kettle what seemed like just minutes later, he said, "Be careful. I boiled the water for you because I thought you'd like your tea right away." That is thinking in advance of what my needs were and meeting them. It wasn't difficult, it cost nothing, but it was thoughtful, and that is the essence of empathetic service.

The ultimate question is: can employees learn this skill or are there only a select few who actually possess it?

In his study of youngsters, Dr. Felix Warneken, associate professor of psychology at Harvard University, observed toddlers as they viewed a person in need, such as someone trying to open a closet door when their hands were full. In the majority of cases, the response was to help the person, engaging their empathy to figure out what was needed. The study proved that everyone is born with empathy, and it's evident up to the age of two or three when societal pressures take over and the child begins to fear being jeered at by peers rather than do what comes naturally.[2]

If we are born with empathy, then, can we re-learn it? Research indicates that adults can tap into their own empathetic side regardless of age.

A famous study by C. Daniel Batson asked two groups to respond to a teenager crying because she just learned she had lost her parents in a tragic car accident. The first group was asked

> In *Empathy: Why It Matters and How to Get It*, Roman Krznaric suggests a number of ways we can reignite our natural empathy[1]:
>
> - Be consciously aware of opportunities to be empathetic regardless of where you are – at work, home, in the grocery store, or walking down the street. This will develop a greater ability to see empathy and activate it when appropriate.
>
> - If you see someone acting in an empathetic way, make a mental note. Acknowledge what they are doing, even if it's just recognizing how they are feeling and experiencing another person's situation.
>
> - Move outside of your comfort zone, including traveling to different places and cultures, which will awaken your awareness. This is especially true in developing countries where customs and practices are often wildly different from those we experience in North America.
>
> - Be curious with strangers and really listen to what they say. Ask questions to find out how they felt in situations and challenge yourself to 'walk in their shoes.'

to report on the facts that were provided. The second group was asked to put themselves in the young woman's shoes, imagine the experience and feelings she would be having, and then verbalize them to the research team.

The second group measured higher levels of empathy. In addition, when a collection was taken for the young lady and her younger siblings to help support the family without parents, the second group gave much more.[3]

DEVELOPING EMPATHY IN EMPLOYEES

With this research in mind, how do you get employees to feel empathy and respond appropriately? How do you encourage employees to think outside the box and say and do things that provide lasting positive memories for a guest?

It starts at the top. A culture of empathy in a hotel begins with leaders who show empathy not only to guests but also to employees. After all, how can you expect employees to be empathetic and respond with compassion toward guests if they aren't treated that way themselves?

By modeling authentic empathy when interacting not only with guests but with peers and employees, leaders can show employees how it's done. It sets the standard for expectations. What is key is that empathy kicks in when you start to get to know someone not only as a face in the crowd or a room number, but as a human being and as an individual with good days and bad days. The more leaders see their team from this perspective, the more they model the behavior of empathy.

What does this look like? Here are just a few examples to consider:

After a conference service manager works six fourteen-hour days in a row, at the beck and call of a demanding meeting planner, her boss gives her a three-day long weekend. During her absence, the boss handles any issues without bothering her.

An employee advises his manager that his wife has just been diagnosed with cancer. The empathetic manager finds out the schedule for the treatment and calls the employee afterward to see how everything went. The manager proactively reaches out to discuss juggling the employee's schedule to take his wife's treatments into account.

A member of the housekeeping staff has a baby. The supervisors and directors visit the staff member and welcome the new baby to their family.

It's five days before month-end, and a finance clerk's computer is showing signs that it's about to give out. The manager brings in a new computer and works with IT to load all the software and reports before the old one breaks down and creates a crisis for the employee.

That is empathetic leadership in action.

> *"Just as empathetic service means anticipating the needs of guests, empathetic leadership means anticipating the needs of employees and meeting them proactively."*
>
> JO-ANNE HILL

It is also true that certain people are more naturally empathetic and aware of other people's feelings. Given its importance in service delivery, identifying candidates during the hiring process who have this gift already is an advantage and will help to raise the level of awareness with the entire team if it is allowed to blossom under a great leader.

TREAT EMPLOYEES AS YOU TREAT GUESTS

Not so long ago, leaders were cold and distant, barking out orders to employees while being charming, warm, and welcoming to guests. Happily, those days are largely gone. There is now an expectation that leaders treat employees the same way they treat guests.

This principle is the foundation of everything I espouse in my work with hotels and their leaders, and I will revisit it in different forms in later chapters.

> There is often confusion between empathy and sympathy. Empathy, as described above, is walking in someone's shoes, understanding and potentially even feeling what they are feeling. Sympathy is feeling sorry for someone. It may be commiserating with them, which may be appropriate in some cases. However, it is not imagining yourself in their situation with the corresponding feelings and emotions.

COMPASSION

Compassion might be defined as the action taken as a result of empathy. This might mean placing a framed picture of a guest's children beside the bed when they are out of town on business or supplying a fresh tube of toothpaste when the current one is almost empty.

Wharton School management professor Sigal Barsade found that engaging with co-workers about their families or weekend activities is vital to employee morale, teamwork, and customer satisfaction. He defines this as "companionate love" in the workplace. Clinical studies found that it reduces absenteeism and burnout, and organizations with a culture of companionate love had higher levels of employee engagement.[4]

A study of healthcare providers found that the culture of companionate love rippled out from staff to influence patients and their families. The study also looked at other industries such as real estate, finance, and public utilities, and the results were identical even for industries not known for their compassion. A culture of companionate love positively correlated with job satisfaction, commitment to the company, and accountability for performance.[5]

Recently, I overheard a breakfast server say she brought in some fresh fruit that she picked from her garden to share with another server. That simple act is companionate love in action.

Compassion in action need not be dramatic to have an impact. Four Seasons Los Angeles was the location for a day-long wedding event, starting with a rehearsal followed by the actual ceremony and then a dinner. The wedding party, decked out in their finery, went through the brief rehearsal that preceded the 'real' wedding without a hitch. Then things went awry when a gust of wind knocked down the chuppah (the canopy the couple and family stand under during a Jewish wedding ceremony) right at the time when everyone was under it. The groom suffered a cut above the eye, the father of the bride also had cuts, and the wedding dress seemed to be a magnet for the blood.

Immediately, the hotel manager kicked into gear and used the hotel car to get people to a clinic for stitches. The bride was whisked downstairs to the laundry department where her couture gown was painstakingly sponged clean to perfection.

All the while, guests were arriving, and apologies were made. Within the hour, the wedding ceremony resumed with a radiant bride in a spotless white gown.

During the evening speeches, the father of the bride publicly thanked the Four Seasons for rising to the occasion and turning a possible catastrophe into a time of bonding for both families. The prompt and compassionate response by the hotel manager and employees in various departments averted disaster on one of the most important days in a family's life and created loyal customers for life.

Providing compassion in everyday life has an additional benefit to the person giving compassion. Studies have shown that when we regularly show compassion, it not only makes us feel better but also has the physiological effect of lowering blood pressure and can add years to our lives.[6]

Acknowledging the importance of empathy is only the first step in working toward creating a great service environment. Leaders must model empathy with guests and staff every day.

Are you creating an empathetic and compassionate environment?

1. Roman Krznaric, *Empathy: Why It Matters, And How to Get It* (New York: Perigee Books, 2014).

2. Felix Warneken and Michael Tomasello, "The Roots of Human Altruism. British Journal of Psychology" (first published: May 11, 2011), https://doi.org/10.1348/000712608x379061.

3. C. Daniel Batson et al, "Empathy-Induced Helping Due to Self-Other Merging," accessed May 3, 2108, https://www.researchgate.net/publication/247434729_Is_Empathy-Induced_Helping_Due_to_Self-Other_Merging.

4. Sigal G. Barsade and Olivia A. O'Neill, "What's love got to do with it?", *Administrative Science Quarterly, 2014.*

5. Human Resources Research, Focus North America, "Why Fostering a Culture of Companionate Love in the Workplace Matters", Wharton/University of Pennsylvania, accessed December 5, 2014, http://knowledge.wharton.upenn.edu/article/fostering-culture-compassion-workplace-matters/.

6. The Center for Compassion and Altruism Research and Education, "Conversations on Compassion with James Doty, MD, and Thich Nhat Hanh" (lecture, Stanford University, October 24, 2013).

"You can have great customer service without it being an experience, but you can't have a great customer experience without terrific service at the foundation."

JO-ANNE HILL

LEADERSHIP AND THE CUSTOMER EXPERIENCE

Ever since the 1990s, as more and more hotels have entered the market offering little difference in physical product, hotels have begun focusing on experiences to be unique or to differentiate themselves from others. At the same time, guests want a more curated visit based on what is important to them as individuals and will give them the greatest value for their time and money. What they choose to do is a reflection of themselves, and affluent travelers especially want to go deeper into this discovery. No longer does one size fit all. A key reason that Airbnb has become so popular is that guests have the ability to interact with their host, typically a local person who is 'in the know' and gives the inside scoop on what to see, eat, and do that might not be found in a travel book.

It's these bespoke experiences that explain the incredible popularity of Fogo Island Inn in Newfoundland, Canada. Zita Cobb created a destination in a forgotten fishing village. She hired a world-class architect, who also was a former resident, who designed an iconic structure for the inn, and Cobb filled it with locally made furniture and quilts. She hired a top chef and designed menus based on local cuisine. Cobb also established a foundation for artists and created

FOGO ISLAND INN

> **Customers versus guest**
>
> The use of the word "customer" is more of a sales and marketing term since it refers to the person before they arrive at the hotel. Once they are checked in, they become a "guest," which is a more gracious way of saying "customer." It rolls out the welcome mat as you would to a guest in your home.
>
> There is one exception to this. We talk about "customer service," and it includes when a guest is in-house. However, it is used because it is a universally recognized term anytime someone is serving the public.

four individual studios around the island for artists to live and work in to develop their talent, reviving crafts and artisan heritage on the island and stringing them together in a walking tour, all an easy walk from the inn. This is the type of authentic experiences that customers are looking for.

It's easy to say a hotel offers great customer service, delivering over-and-above experiences and creating positive memories, but in reality, this is rare. In fact, according to a survey by Corporate Executive Board, 84 percent of guests surveyed said that their expectations had not been exceeded in their last customer-service interaction. So, there is an opportunity for operators who get it right.[1]

The hotels who do get it right will be those with the advantage of great leaders who understand the importance, and the commercial value, of the guest experience.

CUSTOMER SERVICE VERSUS CUSTOMER EXPERIENCE

Customer service and customer experience are two different things. Customer service is about being efficient and prompt, and always with a smile. These are technical skills that can be learned through training.

Great customer experience goes deeper, however, and requires an emotional connection between employee and guest. It starts with the delivery of good service as the building block and continues by treating the customer as an individual and customizing the interaction based on their needs at any given moment. It means being empathetic to the needs of the customer, taking cues about how someone is feeling based on what they are saying verbally as well as what they are saying through their body language. The guest's stay is an event and, done correctly, makes a positive, indelible imprint on their mind. So much so that when they remember the hotel, they associate it with warm, positive emotions.

When you arrive at a hotel tired after a long flight, and the front-desk agent quickly and efficiently checks you in so that you are in your room in a matter of minutes, that is good customer service.

But imagine if you heard this: "Welcome back, Mr. Smith. We have been expecting you. You've probably been traveling all day to get here. Is there something I can help you with to help you settle in? Room-service order? Suit pressing?" Treating you as an individual with unique needs and feelings will begin to create this emotional connection.

GUEST EXPERIENCE AS IT SHOULD BE

A few years ago, I traveled to Cancun for a business meeting. Thanks to a delayed flight, I arrived at The Ritz-Carlton in the middle of the night and quickly crashed in my room without dinner or even a snack. When I woke up the next day, I was jet-lagged and ravenous. You know that feeling of disorientation when you wake up in a different place and time zone? That's how I felt.

It was late morning by the time I left my room and went in search of a place to get some food. Breakfast service had long finished, and lunch hadn't really started. The restaurant was empty except for a few employees preparing for the onslaught of the lunch crowd. It lacked atmosphere, and I feared the service experience was going to be devoid of warmth, but it was food, and I was hungry.

The host seated me and gave me the Americanized menu. After a few minutes, the server came to the table to take my order. "I don't see it on the menu," I said, "but would the kitchen be able to prepare huevos rancheros for me?"

Suddenly, a huge smile erupted on the server's face. "You like Mexican food!" he exclaimed with obvious delight, and we made an instant connection. When he looked me in the eye, it was as if the sun suddenly came up and the room became warm and familiar. The blur of jet-lag disappeared, and I felt like I was at home with my family. He recognized my feeling of disorientation and used his empathy to tap into how I was feeling and then overcame it. This emotional bond I had with the server stayed with me for the entire stay.

As a result of that experience, I went back to that restaurant several times during my stay, and I have told that story countless times, always acknowledging that The Ritz-Carlton, Cancun is one of my favorites. It's not surprising that they consistently win awards, as they have embraced a culture of exceeding the guest's expectations.

Customers have more choice than ever before. When faced with choosing between two or more hotels of similar or equal value, the one with the emotional connection based on a positive experience will inevitably win out. The only way to make that a reality is for the hotel leadership to embrace the concept of an experience and regularly highlight opportunities and possible options.

THE 3 P'S OF LEADERSHIP

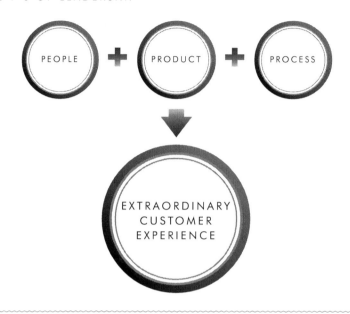

THE THREE P'S OF CUSTOMER EXPERIENCE

1. People

The first step in the customer-experience journey starts with leaders creating an extraordinarily positive experience for their employees. That's because employees must first see and feel it themselves in order to understand what it is, so when the time comes in a moment of truth with a guest, they know what an emotional bond is all about and can effortlessly provide it. This means leaders create a respectful and trusting environment and learn to empathize with everyone. If employees feel this in their own work environment, then they are more likely to pass it on and provide guests with a similar feeling.

To make this happen, exceptional customer service must be identified as a core value of the organization. It must be embraced by the whole organization. It must be championed by the CEO/general manager through regular communication to remind everyone that it is a non-negotiable value for the organization. It must become embedded as a part of the culture and behavior of every employee.

There isn't a manual written that reviews step by step how to deliver positive memories for customers, because it's completely dependent upon the situation and even the needs of the individual customer. The key is to make the experiences happen naturally in the split seconds of an opportunity with a guest. These moments often have a few options for responses, and when leaders have previously provided a foundation or examples, encouragement, empathy training, and recognition, when faced with a situation the employees will then decide with the knowledge they will be backed by their boss, even if from time to time it isn't the best option for the hotel.

Leaders must take an active role in enlivening this core value, showing by example, providing exceptional customer experience whenever they interact with a guest. They should also regularly share examples of customer experience with the team.

Hiring processes need to identify candidates who value customer service and have shown this behavior in the past. Embracing the service attitude means they will exhibit this behavior with customers and fellow employees and evolve to be servant leaders in the future.

The ultimate screening

Before the Four Seasons New York opened in 1993, the pre opening team was inundated with potential employees. Eleven thousand people were screened for six hundred available positions. What did they use as a screening process? A smile. Candidates who smiled when they approached the reception desk for the interview were the ones selected to proceed to the interview process.

Skills such as serving a drink or making a bed can be learned, but a person's ability to smile and be genuine, kind, and thoughtful even when they think no one is looking is part of their core. By selecting the right people based on attitude and providing ongoing skills training, Four Seasons New York has secured its status as the longest-running five-star property in New York.

Regular and ongoing training for every employee must include both technical skills and the 'soft' skills that enable them to read the cues from customers and understand their needs and the appropriate responses. It must activate the natural-born qualities of empathy (understanding and feeling what someone else is feeling) and compassion (responding to those feelings with appropriate words and actions). Empathy exists in young children but is usually lost as they socialize. With awareness and attention by discerning leaders, it can be reactivated.

The leader's role continues by empowering employees to act when the customer presents a need, recognizing and rewarding employees for using these soft skills. If the action is excessive or doesn't quite work, there is no retribution, and it is used as a learning tool for others to encourage similar acts of empathy and compassion.

2. Processes and systems

Working in tandem with the team that delivers the experience are essential processes. This ensures that when an employee learns a guest preference, they record it into a repository that other employees can access when necessary.

The best example of this is the use of a guest name. When room service is able to answer the phone with "Good morning Ms. Johnson, how can I help you today?" the guest is impressed that she is being called by name. Using this technology to record details such as food aversions, potentially life-threatening food allergies, room-location preferences, or even personal information such as the name of their children, helps guests feel their stay is customized to their needs and they are not treated like a reservation number.

But technology doesn't do all the work. When leaders encourage and reward employees for populating and using the information, there will be an increase in usage. For example, when the front-desk clerk asks an arriving guest, "Have you stayed with us before?" it can make the guest feel like a stranger. On the other hand, when technology has been used to record their previous stays, this question can be eliminated. The greeting becomes, 'Welcome Back!' and the employee can move on to more important questions that build on existing engagement.

That's what makes a guest feel like a member of the family. Developing a step-by-step process using systems and employee training will make sure they always do.

Technology can also enhance future stays and be shared with sister hotels. Investing in a solid customer-relationship management (CRM) platform will make this possible, and used correctly it will increase loyalty to the hotel and brand. This tool also allows the hotel to communicate with customers in their preferred medium, whether it's e-mail, newsletters, personalized phone calls, or even regular mail. Top customers should always be the first to know about special offers, even if in the past they have paid more. This will engender loyalty and support of the hotel. See more about hotel processes in Chapter 8.

3. Product – tangible and intangible

The burden of providing this extraordinary customer experience doesn't rest solely on the shoulders of the employees. It also depends, to a certain extent, on the physical product of the hotel.

It used to be that a hotel classification was defined by the amount of marble in the lobby and the size of the guest room bathrooms. Now, however, large bathrooms and the proliferation of marble around the hotel are seen at all levels and are no longer measurement criteria. This has blurred the definition of "luxury."

The term "residential" began in hotels in the '80s, when it was important for hotels to feel comfortable and welcoming, like your home. In recent years, we have moved away from that term because it is no longer valued by the guest. Many guests have much grander homes or completely different décor taste, so it may not feel like their home at all.

What is important in hotel design décor is that it is comfortable, welcoming, accessible, functional, and tasteful. The design must be current, fresh, and in keeping with the hotel niche or position within the marketplace. Add to this the fact that it gets a lot of wear and tear, making the interior design of a hotel very complex.

In recent years, a new element has been added to the mix: a sense of place that reflects the location, whether it's Bali or London or Tokyo. This allows the hotel physical experience to begin well before someone enters the lobby, perhaps at the front door or even the driveway. It helps create a wonderful experience of staying or dining at the hotel, and not just a bed and shower or dinner.

This experience comes in many forms and may include free events in the lobby that are unique to the hotel, or employees engaging so deeply with guests that they return just to continue that relationship. Examples of events include:

- a Hungarian handicraft fair, local musicians, and cuisine hosted weekly at a hotel in Budapest,
- Hawaiian music sung by staff members (in their uniforms) in the hotel lobby, complete with ukuleles, every Friday,
- evening 's'mores on a stick' around a fire pit in Arizona, and
- "I left my heart in San Francisco" is the on-hold music at a San Francisco hotel when someone calls the hotel and is waiting to be transferred to another extension.

Developing unique experiences that reflect the local environment sets the hotel apart from the competition, even if they are subtle and in the background. If done well, these experiences change the hotel from merely a building to a living environment with a pulse, leading to an emotional connection and engagement between the hotel and the guest.

Taking part in these special programs and events (like the Hawaiian music) might not come easily to some staff. Leaders can make it safe and comfortable for them, perhaps by taking part themselves, and even better if they aren't very proficient at it, since it shows the leaders' human side and their ability to laugh at themselves and have fun with their team.

INNOVATION AND CREATIVITY

In this context, it's vital for leaders to spearhead and even create an environment of innovation, encouraging out-of-the-box ideas on ways to improve the service experience. The first rule of inviting ideas is to consider each one, however wacky, and the second rule is to try to implement as many as possible. Adhering to these two guidelines will encourage more people to come forward with ideas. Consider rewarding the good ones and acknowledge even those that may not be as great, because you never know when they might spark an idea from someone else.

Often, it's the employees who are interacting with guests every day who have the best ideas. I've seen innovation in action at hotels when leaders were not aware of issues with supplies and weren't proactive at purchasing or ensuring prompt delivery of linen. Left on their own, employees came up with some amazing 'work-around' plans to make sure the guests weren't inconvenienced, whether by lack of teaspoons for a banquet or linen supplies to service a guest room; even asking guests to e-mail reservation details to avoid making a mistake. Imagine harnessing this creativity and using it to develop memorable experiences versus figuring out how to do their job with limited resources.

Recently, a stay at the Statler Hilton at Cornell University proved exactly that. Hotel leaders created a program of implementing students' ideas and acknowledging them in the guest rooms. One student's innovative idea was to provide a cloth bag in the guest room to collect conference material the guest didn't want. The hotel would donate it to a charity on the guest's behalf. I donated a conference water bottle and knapsack. What a great idea! Someone in need would benefit from it, and I didn't need to carry it all the way home only to throw it away.

HOTELS AS LEADERS IN THE COMMUNITY

Hotels also have a responsibility as members of the community in which they reside to be more than just commercial enterprises. In fact, they need to serve the community by being responsible and respectful.

For example, they need to be aware of excess or after-hours noise, cooking smells, traffic congestion, parking options for guests, frequent garbage pick-up and dealing with unruly patrons even when they are outside of the hotel building.

Going one step further, hotels that are truly part of the community, participating in important events and community interests, are the ones that benefited most with local support of their restaurants and banqueting facilities, not to mention positive comments and recommendations from taxi drivers.

Leaders of new hotels have an opportunity to establish this community involvement right from the beginning when a hotel is being built and maintain it throughout its life.

Looking at a hotel as a holistic unit, those who have employees who are welcoming to guests and non-guests, leaders and team members who love serving others, a warm and approachable physical environment, a position as a respected and involved member of the community, and a clearly defined and accurate position that describes the uniqueness of the hotel will result in financial returns that exceed expectations.

Add a great location to this mix, and the hotel will have no excuse not to be hugely successful!

While I have never seen a hotel that has all the above going for it, what is within the control of the hotel leadership is the human component. With extra attention by leaders, this element can overcome a secondary location and less-than-ideal physical plant.

This book is written for leaders of hotels like this and is a prescription for making a hotel not only successful and profitable but one where everyone recognizes it the minute they walk through the lobby doors.

An extraordinary customer experience can come in many forms, and the only surefire way to make it happen is with leaders who not only make it a priority but also embed it in their own behavior with guests and, even more importantly, with members of their own team and other staff. This is the key to unlocking extraordinary experiences for customers. Getting the right team, encouraging innovation, developing processes, and working with the physical product will be the building blocks once leaders build the foundation.

There are endless possibilities for hotels to provide experiences that go above and beyond. These are the hotels customers want to be part of, and they are willing to pay more for the experience and go out of their way to be there.

1   The Corporate Executive Board Company, "Shifting the Loyalty Curve: Mitigating Disloyalty by Reducing Customer Effort," 2009; accessed March 11, 2018, https://www.marketingfacts.nl/images/vacatures/Shifting_the_Loyalty_Curve(B2C).pdf.

> "Most people take culture as a given... I find that when you champion the most noble values...employees rise to the challenge, and you forever change their lives."
>
> ZEYNEP TON
> *THE VALUE OF HAPPINESS:
> HOW EMPLOYEE WELL-BEING DRIVES PROFITS*[1]

– 6 –

SHIFTING THE PARADIGM: LEADING AN EMPLOYEE-CENTRIC HOTEL

A ccording to a study by the US Travel Association, one in nine jobs depends on travel and tourism.[2] While many hospitality employees are university graduates, it is also an industry in which people with lower levels of education gain employment, a steady paycheck, and a sense of pride in their work. Crucial to achieving a successful organization today and into the future is changing the paradigm to focus on the people who serve the guests, leading with soft skills such as care, compassion, empathy, and grace — in other words, with humanity.

THE PEOPLE COMPONENT

1. Customer-less
2. Soul-less
3. Head-less
4. **Maximizing the People Component**

People taking care of people: when leadership cares for employees, engaged employees care for customers, and customers respond in turn by consuming more of the product. This cycle starts with becoming employee-centric.

Employees are the ones interacting with guests every moment of every day. They are the face of the organization and its brand and have an impact on the guest experience that often goes unrecognized. These men and women are regularly interacting with guests, usually having the first encounter with them in reservations and providing the last impression via the front desk or doorman. Leaders, on the other hand, usually interact with guests just a handful of times of the thousands of guest encounters in a given day.

Jan Carlzon, the former CEO of SAS Group, refers to these encounters as "moments of truth." According to Carlzon, there are fifty thousand moments of truth every day in which a positive or negative interaction can determine whether a customer will return or not or spread the word about their experience. He cites these interactions as a determining factor in whether the organization succeeds.[3]

Acknowledging this simple truth, the importance of a positive interaction between a guest and an employee is paramount to a successful operation. The key question is, how do you motivate, inspire, and challenge employees to serve the public with all its idiosyncrasies, bad habits, bad manners, and inconsiderate behaviors? To perform sometimes mindless repetitive functions in a timely manner, adhering to management or brand standards, and in some cases physically demanding work, all while remaining enthusiastic, motivated, and empathetic?

People typically aren't able to do this themselves. They need to be led there, to follow in the footsteps of leaders who model the desired behavior.

When Isadore Sharp, one of the acknowledged leaders of the entire hospitality industry, began Four Seasons Hotels and Resorts in the '70s, he implemented the golden rule: "Do unto others as you would have others do unto you." When I spoke with him about the success of Four Seasons, he told me this became the organization's culture. Its leaders embraced the mantra of treating employees well, shifting the dynamics from authoritative order-giving to a collaborative, caring approach.

What's particularly interesting about the golden rule is that every major religion, from Buddhism to Christianity to Islam to Judaism, and so on, embodies a similar concept. Looking at it from the universal perspective, people, regardless of how similar or different, can work successfully together if they treat each other with mutual respect, dignity, tolerance, and trust. This principle is applicable around the world and is still as relevant today as it was when Isadore Sharp and Four Seasons introduced it to the hotel industry over forty years ago.

The concept of employees at all levels playing an equal role is also embedded at Ritz-Carlton with its motto, "Ladies and Gentlemen serving Ladies and Gentlemen." Each employee is an equal to each other and the guests, underscoring the British tradition of hospitality as a noble profession. It also guides leaders to treat employees respectfully as equals.

When leaders treat their employees as they treat guests, they consistently interchange the labels of guest and employee with those of person and human being.

A hotel is a microcosm of a city. This is especially true in large hotels, with a thousand employees from many corners of the world and skills as varied as those of culinary master, carpenter, ambassador, painter, salesperson, and cashier. We can now add to the list the recent elevation of technical gurus such as technology managers, revenue directors, and digital marketing managers. The need for all these different skills and personalities to effectively communicate, exchange ideas, and collaborate on how best to serve the guest is even more important today than in the past.

Leading this disparate group of people is not for the faint of heart and comes with its daily challenges and frustrations, which may reduce over time but never go away. While the core tasks remain constant, the complexities that make up each individual — employee and guest — vary like the weather and are just as difficult to predict or plan for. Keeping in mind the big picture and overall goal will help leaders remain grounded.

On a recent trip to Belize, where I was headed to consult with a resort hotel, the airport taxi driver gave me a metaphor that simply and easily describes the interdependence of people working and living together in tolerance and respect.

"Take your hand," he said as he took one hand off the steering wheel and held it up as an example. This wise man went on to explain that each finger is different, but they all have a purpose. The thumb is the most important because it works in opposition to the fingers and allows you to grasp things. The index finger is good with fine movements and is used with the thumb to hold a pencil or pen for writing. The middle finger is the longest and strongest and is the center of the hand. The ring finger is the least useful; however, it

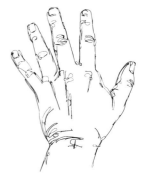

supports the actions of the other fingers. Even the smallest, the 'pinky' finger, increases the range of motion and has 50 percent of the strength of your hand.

While all are different, they each have a role and work together to pick up a book, play the piano, catch a ball, or serve a drink. Without one finger, many functions would be very difficult. They all work together with one goal and support each other to get something accomplished.

This is the type of collaboration that is needed for teams to succeed: the acceptance of differences with tolerance, respect, and trust.

LESSONS FROM THE FIELD: THE POWER OF A UNIFIED TEAM

Let me tell you about three hotels that demonstrate the power of people working effectively together to create success.

Hotel #1

"We worked hard, and we played hard" was the statement from many of the employees at hotel #1. During the tenure of one employee I spoke with, it was listed as one of the top employers in the country, often held the #1 position in average daily rate and RevPAR in the marketplace and the country, and achieved some of the highest customer-satisfaction scores for a luxury hotel company.

What did they do?

The leadership team was run like a tight ship. The executive committee challenged each other in meetings, even on subjects outside their area of responsibility. They all cared about the hotel, and this passion broke down any silos with the ultimate goal of taking care of the guests and employees.

Of course, there were disagreements and lively discussions; however, when they left the meeting, everyone was aligned. Information was communicated quickly, positively, and consistently by each executive to their team, which meant that every employee heard the same thing throughout the hotel.

The executive team was diverse in age, gender, experience level, and where they came from, leading to greater tolerance and understanding for each other, guests and employees.

Around the hotel, successes were celebrated together. Failures were reviewed privately but in an understanding and succinct way. Expectations were clearly rolled out. There were no questions — at this hotel, you knew where you stood.

But most importantly, the employees had fun. Leaders recognized that working long hours and going above and beyond for every guest takes its toll, and one of the best ways to keep that energy and passion going is to provide opportunities for employees to let off steam. Employee-morale budgets were high and liberally used. They took employee parties to a new level, with regular events at which employees gave performances, usually as a department together — with or without talent! Team members and leaders made themselves vulnerable and did it for the fun of it all. The role of perfectionist was reserved for on-the-job with guests.

Hotel #2

Hotel #2 was a traditional hotel with a wide variety of guest room shapes and sizes and small bathrooms. New hotels had arrived in the market with all the latest technology, conveniences, and trends, and all the existing hotels had completed major renovations. The downtown core had shifted so that the location of hotel #2, once considered prime, was now seen to be slightly out of the way and, due to new road patterns, inconvenient to get to.

Corporate travel to the city had also shifted, with a much younger traveler becoming the norm. This was also seen in the leisure travel segment, which was increasingly becoming younger couples, often with children. Both target markets preferred the new hotel options with larger bedrooms and bathrooms.

On top of all of that, the hotel was becoming very tired and in much need of a major renovation.

What did they do?

After six months of underperforming market share reports, the general manager acknowledged there was a problem, and she brought together the executive team to figure out how to solve it. She had an idea of the solution but wanted the people who were going to be implementing the plan and making the necessary changes to come up with it and possibly have a better idea.

The general manager surrounded herself with the best leaders and employees in the business, those who were willing to tackle difficult situations, including the most ardently complaining customer, with poise and grace.

She empowered employees to put people first and allowed them to make decisions regarding rebates and apologies.

At meetings, she motivated the team and inspired them to go above and beyond to do their best.

Her open door meant that she had the pulse of what was going on and took regular walks to see for herself what was happening in every area of the hotel — with all the executive team tagging along for a unified message. Every team member felt cared for and understood that the general manager had their best personal interest in mind as well as those of the guests.

This is an example of a great leader at the top. In addition to having a solid vision, which was developed in tandem with the executive team, the general manager communicated that message constantly and used it as a reference point when decisions needed to be made or explanations were required.

As a result, the hotel improved market share (even without a renovation) and had the highest employee-engagement scores in the company, often achieving similar results for guest-engagement scores.

Hotel #3

Hotel #3 was a city hotel in a resort destination with a healthy balance of individual business travel, group business, and leisure travelers who liked to be close to the nearby shopping mall. However, as new competitors began to arrive on the scene, boasting the full resort amenities of multiple restaurants, different sizes and shapes of pools and lounging areas, and a physical design that shouted "resort," hotel #3 needed to readdress its dwindling leisure and corporate transient business.

What did they do?

The executive team gathered market intelligence to understand what the hotel playing field would look like in three, five, and ten years. Then they objectively viewed the hotel from the customer's perspective, asking themselves what market and customer they best served. Employees who interact with guests were invited to discussions to share firsthand what the guests were saying. Employees were also asked for their suggestions on what the hotel needed to do to improve performance.

Sometimes the answers weren't what the leaders wanted to hear. One of the keys was that the hotel had lost touch with the casualness of the guests and were unbending in the formal dress code requirement for employees. Relaxing the executive team's dress code would exemplify a more relaxed approach to service that was desired by the changing guest.

Armed with lots of data points, the team brainstormed on what success looked like for the future and, most important, how to get there. A comprehensive plan was created.

The easy part was determining that hosting mid-size corporate meetings was the direction to go. The hard part was figuring out how to make sure that they won the business over the 'all singing, all dancing' resorts. Those Goliaths (and, unfortunately, there were many) targeted all sizes and types of meetings to fill all their rooms.

Where this team excelled was in coming together and brainstorming innovative ideas for meeting and event experiences that were out of the box. It was not just coming up with the ideas; it was the implementation and execution that led to the success of this shift in strategy.

Leaders communicated the vision to all employees, sharing the journey of how they came up with the new direction, why it was important, and the role of each employee from the executive committee to the room attendants. It started with a series of town halls that were led by the general manager and over a series of two days, all employees heard the same message, including the night shift. It was carefully scripted so that everyone would hear the vision pared down to three simple points. The meeting needed to be interesting and stimulating since many hotel employees (such as housekeeping and kitchen staff) typically aren't sitting during the day.

At that point, each department head discussed with their team the implications for their department of the new direction. This was done in the form of brainstorming so that each employee felt engaged and heard in the process.

The message was reinforced weekly with consistent communication at morning meetings for the next three months.

Employees were empowered to make decisions, and management would stand behind whatever decision they made. The GM was able to inspire the team to work together, supporting them even if they sometimes got a bit carried away. For example, one employee overheard a guest mention that they loved red roses and then ordered a dozen long-stemmed roses delivered to their room. Even the guest commented that it was a bit overboard, especially since it was a one-night stay. However, the GM supported the expenditure.

Everyone came together when a customer was on a site inspection with a view to business that was consistent with the new strategy.

When sales contracts were signed, an announcement was added to the daily communication, and the whole hotel celebrated and congratulated the sales team for increasing business and keeping the staff employed. If it was an extra-large program, champagne was poured at the weekly department-head meeting. This reinforced the strategy and acknowledged the roles everyone played in making it happen.

Of equal importance, when the hotel didn't win the business it was communicated at department-head meetings in such a way that everyone had the opportunity to learn from the experience.

The result was that Hotel #3 enjoyed one of the highest employee- and guest-satisfaction scores in the company, and they achieved the leadership position in RevPAR in the market.

Be consistent, even (and especially) when under pressure.

A friend of mine outside the hospitality industry recently shared a story that captured the leader's role under stress. A government agency had spent years working on a piece of legislation that was to go to the US House of Representatives for a vote that day. People were under pressure to make sure everything was perfect and submitted in time for the vote. Everyone was excited, but after countless hours, including many late evenings, nerves were frayed.

The leader of the team sent an e-mail to everyone working on the last-minute details. The message was simple: "Take care of each other, support each other, and if you need help, ask."

That simple message quelled some anxiety. Each person could take a breath and realize that taking care of each other was far more important than making sure every "i" was dotted and "t" crossed. To this day, they all feel they are part of a caring team, and even a family, with all the good and bad that goes along with that.

MISTAKES HAPPEN

When mistakes are made, an organization based on trust and respect deals with them in a fair, empathetic, and compassionate way. The discussion is handled in private, in a face-to-face meeting where the conversation is non-threatening and yelling is not tolerated. Each person is asked for their opinion, and their responses are listened to. The process is fair and consistent, as all perspectives are heard.

This is an example of a trusting environment, where all employees know they will be fairly treated when something does not go according to plan. The result is that they will not hesitate to take a risk that would benefit a guest or fellow employee. Even if it is not the ideal decision, it will be reviewed fairly and respectfully.

THINGS THAT GET IN THE WAY: INTERNAL DISRUPTORS

In the hotel business, there has been a lot of talk of disruptors such as Airbnb, which is changing the way customers view hotels. But an even bigger concern is the internal disruptors that get in the way of employees performing their core role and possibly impede their ability to be effective with guests.

The following are three internal disruptions, and there may be more, that are either created or at least exacerbated by leaders. These disruptors can be eliminated or reduced in their impact by forward-thinking leaders who put employees at the center of their management style.

1. One hotel, two designs

An interesting dichotomy exists in the hotel world. At many hotels, the guests' physical environment is much better than that of the employees — a fact that always surprises my non-hotel friends. Non-guest areas, otherwise known as the back of the house, are often very clinical, and sometimes even subpar. With office space at a premium, sales and administrative staff are sometimes stuffed into too-small offices or cubicles.

At one luxury hotel, the sales office so lacked the basic upkeep and maintenance that when it rained, all around the office buckets were set up to catch the rain water pouring in. Over time, the lack of attention meant that mold set in and one of the employees called OSHA (Occupational Safety & Health Administration) to complain about the poor working conditions. That got the leader's attention!

Sadly, this example illustrates a leader who was not employee-centric. The employee complaints about an unsafe working environment that could cause health issues were ignored by leaders, making employees feel they had no recourse but to call in the authorities to resolve the issue. Not caring about employees' basic needs of health and safety had many ripple effects: the distraction of employees stopping work to figure out who to call next, government inspections, lost credibility in the community with future employees and guests, and a complete misjudgment of the value of an employee.

A safe and healthy working environment is a basic right for everyone, but the physical working environment for employees is sometimes undervalued in a hotel.

2. Meetings: too long and too many

> *"For one either meets or one works.*
> *One cannot do both at the same time."*
>
> PETER F. DRUCKER

The very nature of the hotel industry requires a lot of meetings because a guest stay involves so much detailed, intricate information that must be communicated to people in many departments. The current selling rate, for example, used to be simply listed on a whiteboard in the reservations department. It now involves a complex formula that must be clearly communicated to multiple channels and people.

Everything from information regarding a guest, timely updates (such as rate quoting and daily specials in the restaurant), or new guidelines and policies must be conveyed quickly, efficiently, and consistently. Meetings are a vehicle to communicate the information to those involved all at the same time.

Unfortunately, at some hotels team members spend too large a portion of their time in meetings, which takes them away from being with their team, customers, or their basic job function.

At one hotel, the executive committee meeting lasted three to five hours every week! This meant that more than 10 percent of an executive's official work week was spent in one meeting, and that doesn't factor in the barrage of other meetings they were required to attend. Combined with events such as departmental and revenue meetings, one executive on this team determined that they spent 30 percent of their time each week in meetings, which accelerated during budget time. Looking at this from the viewpoint of the financial impact to the hotel, that's approximately $$200,000 of salary time used to sit in a meeting. This doesn't include revenue that could be made if the executive team spent more time leading the team to increase revenue opportunities.

The current management philosophy uses phrases like "scrum" meetings that are short, to the point, and usually conducted with everyone standing, which evolved when employees complained about too many meetings that last too long and aren't productive. They felt that leaders didn't value their time or, by definition, them.

So much time is wasted on unnecessary chatter and background information that doesn't help to solve the issue or is not relevant. This has forced leaders to really think about the purpose of a meeting and create a plan for achieving the goal beforehand versus just showing up like everyone else. It also requires leaders to calibrate when to step into a discussion that is going off topic or is not reaching a resolution. Sometimes leaders need to make decisions even in collaborative environments.

Meetings are essential in a hotel; however, creating a process for clear and concise communication with accountability and controlling drifting discussions will reduce the amount of time leaders are spending away from their employees or guests. Evaluating the content and determining if every member of the team really needs to participate, or creatively determining other ways to share pertinent information without the need for everyone to be physically present, is a step toward eliminating this disruptor.

Effective leaders hold effective meetings. They have a goal, keep everyone on track, and know when to step in to resolve differences of opinion.

3. Long hours

Expecting employees to provide the level of gracious service I've been talking about is impossible if they are tired and overworked due to long hours on the job, and it doesn't help that in some cases there is no additional pay. Individual service providers must be fresh and have basic needs taken care of, such as being well rested, wearing a clean uniform, having personal time to connect with family and friends, and being fairly compensated.

It's interesting that millennials value a balanced life in which they can work a reasonable number of hours and still have time for what is important to them, from meeting friends, to working out, and more. They have seen the downside of overcommitment to work from their parents, who are often burnt out and, in some cases, were laid off after years of unconditional loyalty.

This shift in attitude is a concern to the hotel industry, which for decades has relied on young, eager people entering the industry to work long hours, doing repetitive work.

This expectation that people work long hours in many positions, most notably those in the food and beverage area, must change if the industry is to continue to attract young people. The situation is exacerbated by the continuing influx of more hotels all looking to staff-up their properties with the best and the brightest.

Finally, I want to be clear that I am not advocating the need for organized unions. While throughout history, there may have been a time and a place for them, I am suggesting that strong, effective, compassionate leadership negates the need for employees to organize a union.

At one hotel where I consulted, the leadership team was seen as weak and ineffective. The employees didn't feel taken care of and mistrust set in. The staff turned to the union, who made promises of improved compensation when what employees really wanted was a clear vision, concise and authentic communication, and recognition for extra effort and hours worked for large group events. The hotel changed to a union-represented hotel, and its traditional collaborative working environment changed overnight to us-versus-them.

> *"Tell me what you pay attention to,*
> *and I will tell you who you are."*
>
> JOSE ORTEGA Y GASSET, SPANISH PHILOSOPHER

Pay attention to your employees and treat them just as you would your guests: with grace, empathy, and compassion — in short, with humanity. Take an objective view of disruptors such as the physical environment, unspoken expectations (including hours worked and the quality of meetings), and, most importantly, develop an emotionally effective environment that motivates and inspires everyone to achieve success.

1 Zeynep Ton, "The Value of Happiness: How Employee Well-being Drives Profits," *Harvard Business Review*, January–February 2012, 131.

2 U.S. Travel Association, "U.S. Travel Answer Sheet: Facts About a Leading American Industry That's More Than Just Fun," 85, accessed May 3, 2018, https://www.ustravel.org/answersheet.

3 Jan Carlzon, *Moments of Truth* (Cambridge, MA: Ballinger Publishing Company, 1987).

"Most people take culture as a given... I find that when you champion the most noble values...employees rise to the challenge, and you forever change their lives."

SCOTT COOK
CO-FOUNDER AND CHAIRMAN, INTUIT

GETTING EVERYONE ON THE SAME PAGE: THE IMPORTANCE OF CULTURE IN AN ORGANIZATION

Statistics show that happy and engaged people experience:[1]

- **31 percent** greater productivity
- **37 percent** better sales results
- **34 percent** more positive social interactions
- **23 percent** reduction in stress
- **39 percent** better health
- **Three times** more creativity
- And up to **202 percent** more productivity.

Employee engagement reflects how connected an employee feels to the organization and has recently been embraced by the hotel industry as an important metric. It's a great start to helping to ensure employees are happy and have an emotional connection with the hotel. However, it is just one of the components of the overall health and effectiveness of an organization.

Addressing the culture of an organization takes it one step further and looks at the acceptable behavior and practices of the members of the organization. It brings under the microscope the effectiveness of leadership, distractions from productivity, the strength of processes, and the impact on customers.

Leaders who master these technical components will run their departments or areas of responsibility more smoothly and have more engaged and satisfied employees.

WHAT IS CULTURE?

A simple way to look at culture was developed by Richard Barrett of the Barrett Values Centre, who suggests that culture is defined as "the way things are done around here." The culture is the DNA of an organization and the first place to start to develop and lead any successful endeavor.

Culture takes a holistic approach, viewing the hotel not just as a building but a living, breathing entity. Culture is the basis of everything, the glue that links leaders, employees, and processes together. The effectiveness of this link has a direct impact on the success of the hotel, since it ensures employees are happy, with leaders they respect.

Conversely, the absence of a healthy culture means distraction that has a direct impact on the financial results of the organization. It only makes sense for forward-thinking leaders to explore how to begin the journey of culture transformation.

THE EVER-PRESENT ROLE OF CULTURE

Whether identified, developed, or even acknowledged, every organization has a culture. It is the set of instructions for how the organization works, not the standard operating procedures or best practices but the daily norms and behaviors that are acceptable. Even bad behavior is part of the fabric of the organization if it is tolerated by senior leaders.

However, when positive values such as integrity, trust, fairness, empathy, respect, and extraordinary customer service are embedded into the behaviors and attitudes of the employees, you have the foundation for working together as a team. It makes the team more productive and able to accomplish more without distractions. The more a set of positive values are embraced by employees, the healthier the culture becomes, employee engagement increases, and the sweet spot of increased extraordinary customer experience grows. In this scenario, culture is more defined and relevant and part of the fabric of everyday life.

Customers then see and feel that, and they reward the experience by spending more time there.

THE ROLE OF LEADERS IN CULTURE

The culture is defined by the values and behaviors of an organization's leaders as they set the tone for the culture by:

- How they behave. *Example*: staying in their offices versus walking around.
- What they choose to focus on. *Example*: numbers versus people.
- What they say. *Example*: constantly talking about cost cutting.
- What they condone. *Example*: if stealing is acceptable for leaders, then employees can do it too.
- Their actions. *Example*: at one hotel, it was well known that the GM would walk out the door at the end of each day with a paper cup filled with wine poured from the lobby bar.

In essence, what the leader values is what becomes acceptable behavior. If they tolerate bad behavior or, worse, engage in it themselves, this will become ingrained in the fabric of the organization and become a new standard regardless of how destructive it is.

> *"We are what we repeatedly do."*
> ARISTOTLE

What you spend your time and attention on is what you value. If leaders are spending most of their time interacting with employees and guests, they are showing their belief in the value of relationships, as opposed to leaders who spend most of their time in their offices working on reports.

To put this into perspective, show me someone's credit card statement and I'll tell you what is important to them. For example, if it's full of restaurant expenses with multiple covers, then spending time with their family and friends over a meal is probably what they value. Equally, if there are many diverse high-culture activities such as music concerts and art galleries, then these activities are valued and where this person wants to spend their disposable income and time.

> *"Culture defines everything and motivates everyone."*
> JO-ANNE HILL

Of course, what is written in a mission statement or on the organization's website as the values they uphold, versus the actions demonstrated in daily life, such as interactions and employee behaviors, may be quite different. It's up to the leaders to make sure they are not.

HEALTHY VERSUS UNHEALTHY CULTURES

In a healthy culture, employees and members are happy, engaged, and able to get their jobs completed.

On the other hand, if the attitudes and behavior are negative, they will limit the effectiveness of the organization. In fact, they are often time wasters that lead to fear, mistrust, and low productivity. Unnecessary bureaucracy, confusion, and silo mentality are examples of limiting values, and the Barrett Values Centre identified these specific values as the top recurring limiting (negative) values across North America.

An unhealthy culture can be changed when leaders prioritize its importance and give it constant attention. Once harnessed, culture can be leveraged to unleash the unlimited potential in leaders, team members, and the organization as a whole and lead to exponential revenue growth.

BEHAVIOR DISRUPTORS

There are also subtler disruptive behaviors by employees that, if not addressed, get in the way of getting things done. Gossip, competitiveness, and blame all distract other employees from doing their jobs and lead to a loss of productivity. Whether the whole team is engaged in these types of behaviors or just one disruptive individual, the role of leaders is to observe what is happening and resolve all issues as quickly as possible.

The leader's role is not only to review processes and procedures but also to look at people and behaviors. Just as some procedures need to be reviewed for ongoing relevancy, so too do members of the team. Those who are not a good fit for a collaborative and healthy environment need to be identified and, potentially, removed.

IMPACT OF CULTURE ON THE ORGANIZATION

> *"It's not hard to make decisions when you know what your values are."*
> ROY DISNEY

Just as every society has expected practices and norms of how to act and behave, so every organization has a unique set of accepted ways of doing things, including behaviors that are tolerated or not. Having similar values and clearly defined expected norms takes the guesswork out of an employee's job, which is energy and time that can be directed toward serving guests.

Culture becomes the moral compass of the organization that leaders and employees turn to in determining their actions and is the guidance for executive decisions both small and large.

Employees want to work with bosses and even companies that have values like their own. Aligned values mean employees get out of bed looking forward to coming to work. When they get there, they are with people of similar values, and they bring their whole selves to work. In fact, Lisa Chatroop says in "The High Cost of Unhappy Employees" that 67 percent of employees want their employer to have similar values to themselves.[1]

A strong positive culture means that everyone knows what is expected of them as well as the penalties for not upholding the organization's values. This may result in some employees not accepting the culture, whether it is new or reinforced, and it's best that those employees leave the organization.

A word of caution: once an organization puts a stake in the ground to embrace values and becomes value-centric, leaders need to be constantly aware that everyone will be looking to them and their actions to show the way. While everyone is human, and even senior leadership is vulnerable to transgressions, they hold a new responsibility to do everything possible to live their values both on stage and off.

SEVEN STEPS TO DEVELOP A HEALTHY CULTURE

THE CULTURE TRANSFORMATIVE JOURNEY

The transformation journey toward a healthy culture takes time, attention, and commitment by both leaders and employees, especially when distractions begin to take priority. From working with many organizations to create a healthy culture, I've developed the following step-by-step process to transform a vague, undefined culture into a vibrant, positive, and healthy one.

1. It starts at the top

The key to the transformation process is the commitment of the most senior person in the organization, whether it's the president, CEO, or general manager. Recognizing and embedding the importance of culture as integral to the success of the organization and communicating it constantly in all messaging is the foundation. It then is incorporated into everything, from decision making to recognized acceptable behavior.

The human resources department has a role in institutionalizing it into practices such as hiring, onboarding of new staff, performance reviews, and so on. However, the president must embrace the concept and take ownership to have an impact that truly permeates the whole organization.

For a culture to be strong, all leaders must walk the talk, living the values through their behaviors and actions every day, from formal meetings to casual conversations. All encounters between counterparts, bosses, employees, suppliers, customers, and guests must live up to the values and behaviors even off the clock.

2. What gets measured gets done

Determining a way to measure the culture of the organization is the start of how to get your arms around it. This will provide a benchmark to improve upon, as well as insight into what is really going on.

One assessment that measures culture is a model developed by Richard Barrett, the founder of the Barrett Values Centre, which can quantify an organization's culture in a single number. The top score indicates team members are passionately engaged in what they do, and the organization is healthy. At the other extreme, a score identifying an unhealthy culture means there is disengagement and, at the most extreme, the organization is heading toward a crisis.

In addition, this model has the advantage of identifying:

- barriers to get things done, including the solution to resolve these issues
- the effectiveness of leadership

- the degree of alignment of values between employees and leaders
- the environment employees want, both eliminated and added
- financial viability of the organization, since extremely unhealthy organizations typically fail in the long run.

3. Uncover hidden issues

How one person defines accountability might be something quite different from another employee's definition. Understanding what each person means by each value is critical to figuring out how to improve. Facilitated sessions uncover conflicts or ambiguities in the language and allow for the discovery and bundling together of values that have similar meanings.

This is also an opportunity to have one-on-one discussions with leaders for their perspective on what is happening within the department. Comparing it to how their employees view the health of the same area will determine leadership blind spots that need addressing.

4. Identify the building blocks: core values and mission statement

Leaders define and articulate culture through the organization's core values and mission statements. Refining a laundry list of items into three to five core values that truly represent the organization's beliefs makes them easy for every employee to remember and to refer to as a moral compass. They become the code of behavior for all members of the organization to know and adopt as the way things are done, and they become the building blocks of a healthy culture.

The real acid test for the core values, however, is whether employees see them as relevant, or if they acknowledge them at all. Ask the employees if these represent the real values, beliefs, and acceptable behavior for the organization.

A mission statement goes into more detail as it defines the essence of the business for both internal and external audiences. It often incorporates some or all the core values, but if not, there is a direct connection between the two. While core values are kept to a limited number so that everyone can easily remember them, the mission statement is not required to be memorized but rather used as guidance, especially when challenging issues need resolution.

5. Create a blueprint for success

At this point, solutions begin to surface and lead to an action plan with timelines, accountability metrics, and prioritization so that leaders can tackle the most important issues first and let the 'nice-to-haves' fall to the bottom.

This may require difficult discussions with leaders who are not in tune with the needs of their team or are not behaving in a way that is consistent with the moral compass of the organization. Repercussions for unacceptable behavior also need to be established.

6. Communicate and then communicate again

Since the employees have been asked to share so much insight, the key to success is to share the results and action-plan with them so that they feel heard and responded to. While details about specific employees should not be shared, ideas on how to improve the way work gets done will be embraced even more if all departments discuss the results and brainstorm around how they can improve their areas.

7. Implementation and annual checkup

Conduct an annual survey of team members to understand the progress of the culture-transformation journey and measure the degree to which the core values are embraced by employees and have become embedded in their culture. The follow-up survey, using the initial measurement as the benchmark, will determine if the issues are resolved and if new ones have developed.

Simply giving employees a voice in their workplace is what leading with a heart-centric approach means. It treats people with respect and is paramount in creating an environment of trust. Suppressed opinions, ideas, or undealt-with issues erode trust, and, if not addressed, they lead to employee despondency.

If there is a history of lack of response on issues, suggesting they are falling on deaf ears or, worse, there is a pattern of reprimand for speaking up, fear will begin to infiltrate the organization. Once fear — the opposite of trust — exists, engagement declines, friction, distractions, and chaos increase, employee productivity declines, and all this results in customer dissatisfaction.

At one organization where we began the culture-transformation journey, when we checked back one year later we found the leader had become busy and none of the action plans had been implemented. As a result, 80 percent of the employees who had taken the survey had left the organization. Imagine the impact that had on recruitment time and cost, gaps in customer service, and morale for the remaining staff.

The benefits of moving the culture needle are engaged employees and passionate customers who can't imagine their life without your product or service. It can also affect the tangible results of exponential financial growth, which we will look at in more depth in Chapter 9.

Successful hotel organizations ask their employees for feedback and listen to the answers. Identified values become the moral standard for all to support and adopt. It's a culture of trust, caring, and valuing employees that is driven by leadership from the most senior person on down.

How does your organization stack up on this barometer?

1   Lisa Chatroop, "The High Cost of Unhappy Employees," accessed March 11, 2018, http://archive.is/mK0Yv.

"But the best teams I've encountered have one important thing in common: their team structure and processes cover a full range of distinct competencies necessary for success."

JESSE JAMES GARRETT

– 8 –
THE NUTS AND BOLTS: ORGANIZATIONAL STRUCTURE, PROCESSES, AND STANDARDS

So far, we have talked almost exclusively about a leader's role regarding people. However, it is also the leader's responsibility to define, establish, and implement the infrastructure to help employees do their job. It is the organizational structure that shows who does what, who they report to, who is ultimately responsible, standards required, proven processes to work together, job requirements, and, overall, how work flows. It's these mechanisms — the nuts and bolts — that are often taken for granted in long-established hotels and are sometimes overlooked when systematic change is needed. This often leads to chaos and confusion.

These nuts and bolts can be divided into three sections:

A. Organizational Structure
B. Processes
C. Standards

Leaders who master these technical components will run their departments or areas of responsibility more smoothly and have more engaged and satisfied employees.

What is the leader's role in each of these components?

A. ORGANIZATIONAL STRUCTURE

An easy way to show the structure within the organization is through the organizational chart, which shows the hierarchy of the hotel and specifically who reports to whom. But the organizational structure also defines the roles and responsibilities of each individual, including accountability and even requirements to do the job effectively. It also outlines the staffing levels required to be successful.

Impact of a bad structure

Barrett Values Centre found that 27 percent of North American employees identified confusion within their organization as one of the top barriers to getting things done.[1] A weak organizational structure often means too many people involved in certain tasks and not enough in others. This causes frustrated, unhappy, disengaged employees, which leads to an increase in employee absenteeism and turnover. As we've already seen, disengaged employees result in low productivity, putting revenue and profitability performance at risk.

And it's not only employees who are adversely affected by a bad structure. Gaps in service, from lack of timeliness to poor follow-up or too many people involved in simple transactions, also lead to disgruntled guests.

But serious flaws in an internal operating system go beyond poor service. At the extreme, staff disarray and chaos risk the guest going away for good, with negative impressions of the overall brand cemented in their mind. Ninety-one percent of unhappy customers don't say anything — they just never come back.

An inadequate organizational design also interferes with the integration of new technology and complicates the ability of the company to be scalable for future growth opportunities. If an organization is already in disorder, introducing something new is next to impossible. Correcting the structure, therefore, must be a priority for hotel leaders.

Hotel staffing levels

Staffing levels have always been hotly debated in the hotel industry. Staff is usually the highest expense in a hotel, and leaders need to find the right combination of art and science to reach the optimum level.

It can often be a headache for leaders to figure out the typical production time and anticipate unexpected events that can unhinge the organization. Not only is it necessary to understand the patterns of guests, but it also requires flexibility for out-of-the-ordinary requests — and often life in a hotel is full of unconventional and irregular inquiries.

Room-service requests around the Super Bowl is an example that comes to mind. I remember being at a city hotel miles from the game where people checked in specifically to watch the game in their room and slammed room service all at the same time right after the half-time show. Chaos ensued, and customer complaints were triple the normal level for a weekend.

The rule of thumb for a luxury hotel used to be two employees for every guest room. At resorts, where guests are inclined to use more on-property services such as the spa, pool, golf course, or conference center, the ratio increased to three- or even four-to-one. This meant that when a guest wanted anything, from more towels to a midnight dinner in their room, all were delivered quickly, graciously, and in the case of food, cooked to order.

Keeping optimum staffing levels on an ongoing basis gives employees time to interact and engage with customers to develop a relationship and activate empathy when necessary. The service-delivery person has time to consider options and come to the right decision, rather than be distracted by conflicting priorities that force a rushed decision.

There must also be a process in place to cover sick leave, vacations, or vacant positions, instead of expecting the rest of the employees to pick up the extra work.

A case for organizational structure review

The real issue for leaders is figuring out what is the right number of people doing the right activities to make the organization work efficiently. Whether it's a new hotel, an additional service offering, or replacement of an outdated internal operating system, an effective structure, including the right headcount, is one of the building blocks of employee and guest satisfaction. It gives team members the ability to provide service levels that include going above and beyond to create extraordinary customer experiences.

It defines the tasks, the coordination, and accountability, and it can impact the revenue and profitability of the hotel.

B. PROCESSES

There are thousands of processes that take place throughout the stay of guests: from taking reservations to acquiring guest preferences to ensuring the hotel is properly prepared for their arrival to moving luggage quickly and efficiently to expedite their departure — and a great deal in between. All have potential to break down, frustrating the guest and possibly resulting in the loss of a future stay.

Such a large number of processes, and people who carry them out, requires strong and knowledgeable leaders who effectively interact with their peers to make the entire process seamlessly work.

One major step is to analyze these transactions into process flows to make them work better, reduce errors, limit the number of employees who need to 'touch' the process, and communicate when there are many departments involved. These process flows will make employees more productive and have more time to focus on doing each one right.

In doing this process analysis, it is critical to talk to the people who are doing the work every day. What are the barriers to getting their work done effectively?

Recently at a client hotel, an event planner was complaining that the function room was not set up early enough prior to their big gala dinner. The planner was frustrated that, despite telling conference services they needed access to the room one hour beforehand to distribute their attendee gifts at each place setting, the banqueting staff was still in the room putting down the silverware.

As it turns out, the process broke down because of lack of teaspoons. Because the inventory had dropped, and no one recognized the problem in advance of this large event, the stewarding department was unable to deliver the required silverware for the event until after spoons were cleaned from lunch. The solution was simple: order more spoons. Yet because the process did not work properly, it started the event off on the wrong foot and created unnecessary anxiety for the customer.

There are lots of departments and people involved in making a guest's stay great, requiring relentless attention to effective communication. Clear, concise, constant communication is the foundation of great leadership.

Effective communication by leaders means a regular review of the hotel's performance, upcoming guest programs and events, and guest preferences, as well as clearly defined expectations; all delivered well in advance of the guest arrival. This ensures employees realize the importance of every guest stay

THE 3 C'S OF COMMUNUCATION

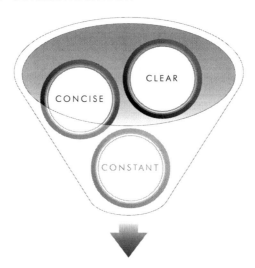

Foundation of a great hotel

90 // Cultivating Leadership

going well and their specific role in making that happen, from the restaurant server pouring the first cup of coffee for a guest at 6:00 a.m. to the bartender serving a cocktail at midnight.

C. STANDARDS

The area of standards covers best practices, brand standards, and all other components that are important to ensure consistency between employees, departments, and hotels within the same organization. Leaders often try to delegate this somewhat tedious responsibility to a junior member of the team or sometimes even procrastinate and eventually ignore it completely.

Standards cover everything from how the beds are made in the guest rooms, to how the phone is answered, to information needed in a reservation to prepare for a guest's arrival. They are often taken for granted in well-established hotels, but from time to time they need to be dusted off to make sure that all the standards are still relevant.

Within this category are also human resources programs such as orientation, onboarding, and disciplinary protocol. The leader's role is to be aware of these programs and be ready to exercise them as appropriate.

THREE STEPS TO ORGANIZATIONAL EFFECTIVENESS

Rather than implementing a Band-Aid solution such as hiring or firing people, the following are my three steps to eliminate chaos and ensure satisfied employees and customers.

1. Follow the guest's journey

Following the journey starts with a deep dive into the behind-the-scenes operational functionality to understand each guest or activity touch point, possible options, the degree of urgency, and the complexity of each activity. A process map follows this journey, charting the people and processes needed to manage each interaction effectively. Leaders need to hold ongoing conversations with staff, and in some cases customers willing to giving their insights, on how information is managed between the customer and the organization and how staff executes each task.

Two different hotel organizations (interestingly on opposite sides of the world) requested that I map the sales process for them to understand where the breakdowns were and how to shorten the response time.

At the first hotel company, we identified ten required steps an individual sales manager had to go through to quote on guest room availability and rates for a meeting. While this process made sure that the quote had multiple eyes and experts involved, they were losing business because meeting planners want fast (and accurate) responses to meeting leads, so much so that 72 percent of the business goes to the first hotel to respond with rates and availability.

Of course, the meeting planner was unaware of all these steps and could never understand why it took so long to respond.

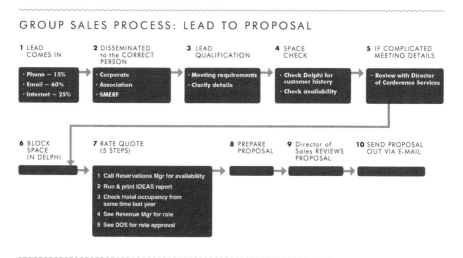

Once we identified these steps and put them all on one piece of paper, the obvious solution was to reduce the number of steps, especially for smaller, less complicated events. It also meant giving sales managers more tools and empowering them to make decisions.

The second hotel company was interested in improving conversion and challenged us to find how to make that happen. While it didn't take ten steps to get a quote, this hotel company had as many as five salespeople speaking to the meeting planner before final rates and availability were provided. This process meant a delay in getting a response to the meeting planner, who was frustrated at having to speak to multiple people, some who were more administrative than sales-savvy. The process itself was resulting in lost business.

By documenting each step and evaluating the process, we were able to combine many of the steps and reassign one of the teams to proactive sales efforts. Reporting lines were also adjusted so that all salespeople reported to one leader and all service people to another. Conversion was improved by 10 percent.

2. Resource allocation

It is important to develop the architecture first and then find people with the necessary skills to complete the tasks, not the other way around. This can be a difficult exercise, especially for a well-established company with good employees already in place.

An objective view from someone outside the company with knowledge of the industry removes the emotional attachment between leaders and employees. It challenges leaders to consider eliminating tasks that are laborious, outdated, and no longer necessary with faster and easier processes as well as empowering the team to make decisions on their own once given the tools and training to make effective ones.

Reviewing the structure will reveal an employee who is no longer productive as a result of lack of training, and this is the ideal time to identify training programs to enhance skills levels to increase productivity. The effectiveness of leaders will also be spotlighted, as limited accountability or lack of clarity will surface as issues.

Leaders implementing a new structure should proceed carefully and incorporate an overall communication plan that starts as soon as the decision has been made to begin the review. The rationale for decisions needs to be explained in detail to staff to get full buy-in and minimize disruption and loss of morale. There is often resistance to change, but leaders who offer a proper explanation, listening to everyone's concerns and responding appropriately, will help staff make the necessary adjustments for a successful transition.

3. Interdependence

The interesting thing about the nuts and bolts of a hotel — organizational structure, processes, and standards — is that they are interdependent. If one area is weak, the whole organism will fail.

A hotel might have the best processes and standards in the industry, but if it doesn't have enough people, the work won't get done, and it will falter. Similarly, if it has the right number of people assigned to fulfill the right roles to meet the needs of the operation but no processes in place, time will be wasted reinventing the wheel each time a guest makes a request.

The same is true for standards since the guest expects certain givens when they check in: a room that is clean and attended to every day, hot water when they turn on the shower, the phone answered promptly, and employees who know what to do when there is a request.

Like a three-legged stool, each of these components relies on the others to do its part to support the person sitting. Take one away, and the stool becomes unstable. It's an interdependent relationship among components, and if one is weak, all the others falter.

Great leaders make sure this happens through regular review and updates. It is this synergistic relationship among these three components that creates an atmosphere of trust and harmony, as well as a hotel that functions efficiently.

RESULTS AND BENEFITS

The organizational structure, standards, and processes are gears that make everything work, and leaders who set it all up properly can free themselves to focus on the people side of service work.

For guests, it means the hotel is 'easy to do business with,' through a caring and eager-to-please staff.

For employees, it means they know their role and are confident that other employees will do their part in creating a product everyone is proud of. They can also count on supportive leaders who have thoughtfully planned and coordinated the smooth transfer from one employee to another.

For leaders, it means everything is documented and held in a central repository where it can be easily found by everyone. It means that new employees and new leaders have guidelines and direction even when the leader isn't there. It means that leaders can be promoted, and the legacy of a well-run department or hotel carries on.

Such an effective organizational structure is a recipe for success. Management is happy with the increase in productivity and lower employee turnover. Employees are happier at work with each member of the team having accountability. Customers are happy and enjoy being part of a well-run establishment where employees go the extra mile to deliver remarkable customer experiences. What more could a hotel leader want?

1   Barrett Values Centre, *North American Region Report* (Summerseat, United Kingdom: April 2014).

"Money goes where it's wanted, and stays where it's well treated."

WALTER WRISTON
FORMER CEO OF CITIBANK

FINANCIAL RETURN

Paradoxically, when senior leaders adopt the 'people first' focus, the company achieves better financial performance. This may be counter-intuitive to some hotel executives who see it as an either/or equation of bottom-line cost effectiveness versus resources spent on training, onboarding, and other culture-based programs.

Focusing on employees, and even becoming employee-centric in priorities and decision-making, will have a direct and positive impact on revenue. In this chapter, I'll illustrate how profitability actually increases when the focus is on employees.

When the primary focus is on numbers and results, rather than on the people who must help achieve them, a company actually underachieves compared to its competitors, as evidenced by the following statistics: [1]

- 70 percent of American workers are *disengaged at work,* resulting in lost productivity valued at over $450 billion per year.
- 89 percent of these failures were due to *poor culture* fit.
- Companies where the majority of employees are disengaged saw their *operating income worsen* by 32.7 percent within the same period.

While these are general statistics, they also apply to hotels and serve as a mirror for hotel leaders to continually examine their own behaviors and results.

Conversely, there are tangible financial benefits when employees come first: [1]

- Organizations with a high number of actively engaged employees have an average of 147 percent *higher earnings per share* (EPS) than the norm.
- Engaged employees are 87 percent *less likely to leave the organization* than the disengaged.
- Companies with a highly engaged workforce have nearly 50 percent fewer accidents.

In addition, according to Gallup, "When companies can increase their number of talented managers and double the rate of engaged employees, they achieve, on average, 147 percent higher earnings per share than their competition." [2]

HOW TAKING CARE OF EMPLOYEES INCREASES PROFITABILITY

In its simplest form, the hotel business is quite straightforward. If customers like their experience, they are likely to spend more while they are there, return again, and tell all their friends about the great experience. Therefore, it's not surprising that those hotels with a high repeat factor make more money.

BENEFITS OF ORGANIZATION TRANSFORMATION

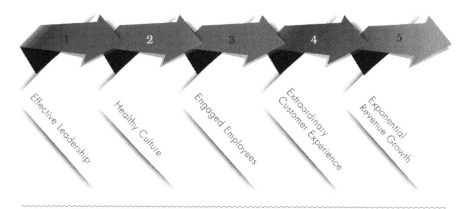

HOW TO INCREASE HOTEL ADR WITHOUT RAISING RATES

From a hotel perspective, engaged employees mean higher Average Daily Rates.

One study found that: [3]

- Given equal prices, travelers are 3.9 times more likely to choose a hotel with higher review scores on such sites as TripAdvisor.

- When hotel prices are increased for hotels with better review scores, travelers are more likely to book the hotel with the higher score despite the higher rate

- When asked, 76 percent of travelers were willing to pay more for a hotel with higher review scores.

The rise of TripAdvisor has meant the objective commentary of guests is a major influencer in travel decisions. While in some cases, it may be an opportunity for dissatisfied guests to rant and possibly exaggerate a situation, astute travelers know to review all the comments for a balanced perspective of the property. A study by Cornell University showed that a higher TripAdvisor ranking meant a higher Average Daily Rate.[4]

By reviewing research from other industries that provide customer service, we can find a variety of data points to support the connection between effective leaders who engage their employees and a positive impact on the bottom line.

In 2008, *Harvard Business Review* republished a 1994 article, "Putting the Service-Profit Chain to Work," and even today, more than twenty years after the original publication date, it is still profoundly relevant. While the model was developed using a variety of industries, it is especially relevant for the hotel industry, which relies on a lot of low- to medium-skilled workers to ensure the care and comfort of guests for many hours or days during their stay.

THE 'PEOPLE FACTOR' IN HOTEL PROFIT

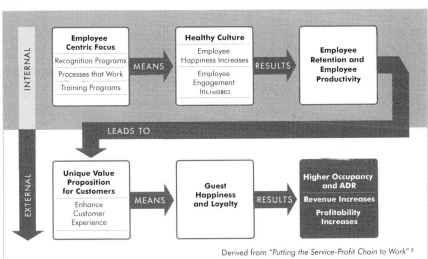

Derived from *"Putting the Service-Profit Chain to Work"* [5]

The premise links employee satisfaction to revenue and profitability in three key ways:

1. **A high degree of employee engagement means higher levels of customer retention.** *Loyal customers* **spend more when they are on-property and come back more often.**

The article found that for every 5-percent increase in customer loyalty, there is a 25- to 85-percent increase in profit.[5] Imagine the financial impact this

Financial Return // 99

has on a hotel once a strategic plan is implemented to get customers to return again and again. In a hotel with $10 million in profit, for example, increasing customer loyalty by just 5 percent will see profits increase by between $2.5 million and $8.5 million. Even if they aren't traveling, loyal guests become key advocates of the hotel to their friends, colleagues, and other like-minded acquaintances.

In a hotel, customer loyalty can be measured in a number of ways: by the amount they spend, including the rate paid and other purchases throughout the hotel, how often they return per year, or even if they just come once per year but in the lowest occupancy month for the hotel. Whatever metric is selected, rewarding and acknowledging return guests for their loyalty will keep them coming back and reduce the risk of them staying at another hotel.

There is a second advantage to identifying loyal guests: determining patterns and rationale for property selection can help to find other guests with the same purpose or preferences. Simply identify the top ten repeat guests, possibly by market segment, and ask them why they stay with you. This simple action will provide amazing insights that will help to find similar customers with the same interests, priorities, and needs.

Is there a nearby office or shopping mall that they want to be close to? Are they going to the opera or a sporting event that has easy transportation access to your hotel? Do they like to entertain in the hotel dining room for breakfast or dinner?

In my consulting practice at various hotels, I often ask these key questions, and I have discovered that while many hoteliers may think they know the answers, asking the guest directly or even the front-office employees usually reveals quite a different answer.

Xerox analyzed customer data comparing satisfaction scores with the probability of buying more of their product. Those customers who rated their experience with a five, the highest level, versus those who only gave a four, were six times more likely to buy another Xerox product. Customers who scored five became brand champions, as they were likely to tell their friends and colleagues about the positive attributes of the service, product, and brand.[5] From a hotel perspective, these are the customers who are likely to write a glowing report on TripAdvisor and will influence many others.

At the other end of the spectrum are the dissatisfied customers, who can be more vocal in the lobby on departure or on social media and can ultimately be very destructive to a hotel's reputation. Typically, unhappy customers tell up to fifteen people about their experience, and 13 percent of them tell more than twenty people.[6] And even more frightening is the 91 percent who are dissatisfied and say nothing but never return.[7]

It's a well-known fact that it is easier and less expensive to get a customer to return than it is to find a new one. Bain and Company has quantified this, stating that it is six times more expensive to secure a new customer than to keep one that you have already.[6] Putting systems in place to make sure the customer is a brand champion may cost more dollars in leadership training, hiring the best person for the job, and ongoing training for everyone, but it is far easier and less expensive than finding a brand-new customer.

2. **An engaged workforce means *lower employee turnover* and *faster replacement time* because prospective employees want to work there.**

"People leave managers not companies…in the end, turnover is mostly a manager issue," Gallup wrote in its survey findings.[7] High turnover results in not only the cost of lost productivity but the cost of recruiting and training. It can often mean lost business because fewer people are available to answer the phone and remaining staff are burnt out. Burnt-out staff who stay but become disengaged can become an even higher cost, as managers are challenged to come up with an effective solution, and the rest of the staff who are around a negative attitude can become stressed also. They are often the ones picking up the extra workload when someone is unproductive.

Happy employees, on the other hand, are less likely to leave. Lisa Chatroop of Good.Co found that the cost to replace an employee was the equivalent of up to 300 percent of their base salary.[1] Taking a salary of $50,000 means that the total replacement cost would be $150,000. If 10 percent of that were spent on training and motivational programs for all the hotel, then this would be reversed and have the benefit of happier employees. The results would go directly to the bottom line.

3. **Engaged employees have *higher productivity*. They want to work for the organization and waste less time on unproductive activities.**

Gallup also determined that teams with weak managers are half as productive and less profitable by 44 percent than those with effective leadership.[7] Drilling down further, wasting time on such activities as gossip, blame, and silo mentality directly corelates to reduced profit. Typically, these activities are a result of leaders who are focused on their own needs or believe that having control or administering from a fear-based perspective is the way to get things done. However, when leaders lead with soft skills such as compassion and create a trusting and caring environment where empowerment, innovation, responsibility, and accountability are encouraged, employee engagement increases and negativity decreases.

Barrett plotted the performance of the best companies to work for in America by share price over a ten-year period (2002 to 2012) compared with the share price of the S&P 500. In addition to outperforming their competitors, with an average annualized return of 16 percent versus 4 percent, employee-centric firms as measured by 'the best companies to work for' were more resilient during the 2008 economic crisis and regained their value faster.[8]

Engaged employees who positively impact someone's stay become advocates, making the hotel more popular. Higher demand results in higher pricing. All of this results in higher revenues and greater profitability.

WHAT TO DO

- Recognize both high employee engagement/satisfaction and guest satisfaction.
- Consider changing incentives from a focus on profit, market share, and RevPAR performance to increasing guest total annualized spend.
- Treat each guest and employee as an individual and celebrate every success.
- Put people first, and financial performance will follow.

Making a profit is, of course, essential. It keeps the business going and the staff employed. It also enables reinvestment in the building to maintain the hotel's relevance and ongoing financial success.

But focusing exclusively on the profit and ignoring the employees and leaders who create the hospitality experience for which customers are going to pay more is detrimental to the business. Focus first on your employees, and profit will follow.

1   Lisa Chatroop, "The High Cost of Unhappy Employees," accessed March 11, 2018, http://archive.is/mK0Yv.

2   Randall Beck and Jim Harter, "Why Great Managers Are So Rare," *Gallup Business Journal*, March 25, 2014.

3   Margaret Ady, "Do Reviews Have An Impact on Hotel Conversion Rates and Pricing?", October 31, 2014, http://www.trustyou.com/blog/miscellaneous/travel-reviews-impact-hotel-conversion-rates-pricing.

4   Cathy Enz, Cornell University School of Hotel Administration, 2016 study.

5   James L. Heskett, Thomas O. Jones, Gary W. Loveman, W. Earl Sasser, Jr., Leonard A. Schlesinger, "Putting the Service-Profit Chain to Work," *Harvard Business Review*, July 2008; Frederick F. Reichheld and W. Earl Sasser, Jr., "Zero Defections: Quality Comes to Services," *Harvard Business Review*, September–October 1990.

6   Colin Shaw, "15 Statistics That Should Change the Business World – But Haven't," accessed March 11, 2018, https://beyondphilosophy.com/15-statistics-that-should-change-the-business-world-but-havent/.

7   Netscape eds., CompuServe Interactive Services, 2014; accessed May 3, 2018, https://webcenters.netscape.compuserve.com/news/fte/quitjobs/quitjobs.

8   Richard Barrett, *The Values-Driven Organization: Unleashing Human Potential for Performance and Profit* (New York: Routledge, 2014) 24–25.

> *"Ultimately, leadership is not about glorious crowning acts. It's about keeping your team focused on a goal and motivated to do their best to achieve it... It is about laying the groundwork for others' success, and then standing back and letting them shine."*
>
> **CHRIS HADFIELD**
> RETIRED ASTRONAUT

WHY IS THIS IMPORTANT? WHY NOW?

There has never been a time when the hotel industry was in more need of great leaders. The industry is in a major period of transition, and maybe even transformation, due to the occurrence of five significant trends:

1. A new generation of graduates and candidates have started to join our industry, demanding a balance between work and personal time, as well as more meaningful work. This is forcing leaders to step back and really look at expectations and, in some cases, reevaluate roles.

2. Overall demographics show more young travelers who require a different environment from the one their parents wanted. This includes mobile apps that allow guests to avoid the front desk when checking in or out and a place to hang out, whether it's the totally wired lobby or rooftop bar.

3. Hotel expenses have increased dramatically in the last few years, with increasing energy and insurance costs, for example. This has caused a dramatic reduction in once-rich training and motivational budgets.

4. Hotel leaders now have a barrage of priorities, from various types of financial reporting to monitoring TripAdvisor comments and social media channels.

5. The industry's model of property owners owning the real estate and the building and hiring a separate entity to manage the hotel operation has meant management companies need to keep finding more hotels to run to grow revenue. In response to this need, management companies have developed a plethora of new brands to have multiple hotels within the same city (and thus avoid territorial clauses in contracts).

It's a new environment, with more competition and more transparency in rates and customer complaints (and compliments) for everyone to see. This makes the job of leaders even more difficult today, since they need to juggle the new dynamics of running a profitable hotel with the soft skills of leading with humanity.

This might seem daunting for some leaders who feel it takes more time to be caring and empathetic or who are more comfortable just giving specific direction and expecting employees to do as they are told.

I've also heard managers espouse the old rules of believing there needs to be a degree of distance from their teams. For them, managing a team means not showing their human side, and certainly not admitting when they have made a mistake. For these people, the transition to an employee-centric approach might be viewed as a quantum leap into something that they don't believe is part of their DNA. I encourage those leaders to consider taking small steps and working toward finding their own approach that, while still tapping into their heart, is authentic for them.

The concept of taking care of the employees first, giving them a voice in the work they do, and treating them like guests isn't new. In fact, I remember a general manager telling me about this idea when I first started my career many years ago. However, I continue to be surprised to hear employees complain about weak, ineffective leadership. Why does this continue in a time when great employees are hard to find, keep, and train?

The ongoing journey requires daily communication, constantly reminding leaders of their critical role and possibly new habits required when leading from the heart. It starts with identifying the core values and a mission statement that is the soul of the organization, communicated in every internal memo, town hall meeting, staff meeting, and even impromptu stand-up scrums.

SUCCESSFUL HOTELS ARE DOING THIS NOW

At one hotel, I saw this principle in action. This hotel was undergoing a transition from having leaders who were rarely promoted and a general feeling that working there was merely transactional, to a hotel where people cared about each other, from the general manager to employees and guests.

Under the new leaders, once a week during the morning briefing, one employee was asked to share an example of enlivening a core value of the organization, either with an example of something they did themselves or something they saw another person do. If no examples were readily available, they personalized what that value meant to them and why it was important to the hotel.

By sharing more personal insights and interpretations of values that were espoused by the organization, they could show the rest of the employees that working there was more than just a paycheck to them, and leaders were personally vested and interested in making this a great place to work. Employees began to embrace this themselves. Promotions from within increased and turnover dropped.

Senior leadership must embrace a relentless commitment to these values. In fact, the only way it will be effective is if it goes right up to the C-suite of a corporation or general manager of a hotel. If these values are not honestly and authentically embraced as the norm, employees will see through the charade, and the entire concept will fail, regardless of the hours of discussion, planning, meetings on the topic, and allocated resources. Team members must see leaders who walk the talk and own the values as a way of life.

Isn't this a great deal of new responsibility for hotel leaders? Not only do they need to modify their actions at work to reflect these values and incorporate them as part of their vernacular, but they also need to 'be' the espoused values even when no one is watching and when things start moving quickly during a crisis or when emotions run high.

Certainly, this is a challenge for leaders, but it's a challenge great leaders wholeheartedly embrace.

Think for a moment of a mundane situation such as driving home from work. It's rush hour after a long day, and you are late for dinner. Someone is trying to move into your lane, someone who obviously jumped the queue while you patiently waited your turn to exit. What is your response? Do you let them in ahead of you, which means that you are potentially even later for your time with your family?

Maybe they believe it's a waste of time to wait in line and don't care about social politeness and graciousness — maybe they're just a jerk. But maybe not. What if they are rushing their child to the hospital after a bad fall? How do you react now?

By switching your mindset to one of nonjudgment of others, going into your heart versus your head, and focusing on your own response, you will save yourself frustration and ultimately live longer.

Now switch this mindset to how you run your hotel. Of course, things don't go well all the time, but getting back on track is yet another responsibility of the leaders. Instead of playing the blame game, why not assume everyone is bringing their 'best self' to the situation every minute of every day, and there is a reason they are acting as they are? More importantly, are you acting and behaving every minute of every day by the values you claim?

Truly embracing these values means a lifestyle shift. They will be tested the most during a crisis or other difficulties when our authentic self is challenged.

As discussed earlier, people like to work with other people of similar values. They like to work with like-minded people. If your hotel is focused on valuing employees, providing empathic leadership in an environment of trust and respect, then you will attract other employees, vendors, and suppliers who feel and act the same way.

Customers also want to affiliate themselves with organizations that have a similar belief or value system to their own. Consider the Harley-Davidson brand. Harley owners become brand evangelists when they permanently tattoo the logo on their arms. Apple has a similar following of committed customers who have stayed with them through the company's life cycles, even when it was on the brink of going away.

A hotel with a soul still has a responsibility to provide owners with a return on investment but also a responsibility to the surrounding community, providing jobs, paying taxes, and making the community better by playing their part as an integral component of the community at large.

What does this look like? It means supporting the community by extending the hand of caring, empathy, and compassion. In Santa Monica, California, it's donating used blankets and even new ones to a homeless shelter. In Toronto, Canada, it's supporting Ronald McDonald House with annual spring cleaning by the hotel management team. In London, England, it's donating 10 percent of all hotel revenue to campaigns in Africa to save elephants. These are all examples of corporate responsibility and of organizations that view their responsibility beyond just the building and team that they inhabit.

And while these activities may sound like just nice-to-dos, leaders who support these types of endeavors not only increase the esprit de corps within the organization but also bring increased exposure and awareness to their community. What initially appears to be an additional expense with no return becomes an activity that actually increases revenue and profitability.

Happiness is also contagious. Whether it is in a social activity or work environment, when a happy person interacts with someone else, not only does the other person become happier, it then affects the next person that person comes in contact with.

Everyone is happier, from employees to leaders to owners, and, like ripples in the lake when a stone is dropped in, the impact extends to customers.

That impact is also felt at home with the families of employees and surrounding neighbors. When someone has a great day at work, they go home and share the care and compassion that they received with their family and friends. Working and living a value-centric, heart-centered, humanity perspective can change the entire world. The world becomes a better place to work and live.

Building an organization from scratch with this perspective is obviously the ideal for developing a values-centric organization. However, for some hotels, this requires a transition from an old way of thinking, and organizations change only when their people do. Fortunately, with leaders' unrelenting commitment, discipline, and patience, an organization's culture can shift, and negative forces can be reduced or eliminated.

Embracing an employee-centric, humanity-based approach that listens to and takes care of employees gives those employees a voice in the workplace. It's providing leadership in a way that treats employees as the unique human beings they are while still recognizing the need to get the work done.

And of course, leaders of profitable hotels, where engaged employees provide superlative service to ever-growing numbers of delighted guests, automatically become happier themselves. Why wouldn't they?

That is, after all, why you and I chose to be in the hospitality business.

WHY THE PINEAPPLE?

For centuries, the pineapple was seen as a symbol of welcome and hospitality. It started when early explorers discovered the Caribbean tradition of displaying a pineapple at the village entrance to welcome visitors. On their return to Europe, explorers introduced the exotic fruit to European society, and its welcoming significance remained. In the 1600s, King Charles II of England commissioned a portrait of himself receiving a pineapple, and even into the 1960s pineapples adorned dining tables as welcoming centerpieces and an enduring symbol of hospitality even today.

Made in the
USA
Middletown, DE